W9-CEU-552

400 SL

A Culinary Collection

FROM THE METROPOLITAN MUSEUM OF ART

A Culinary Collection

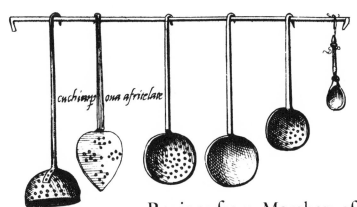

Recipes from Members of the
Board of Trustees and Staff of

The Metropolitan Museum of Art

Compiled by LINDA GILLIES
ANITA MULLER
PAMELA PATTERSON
Edited by LINDA GILLIES

THE ILLUSTRATIONS are taken from an early Italian cookbook, *Il Cuoco segreto di Papa Pio V* [*The Private Chef of Pope Pius V*], by Bartolomeo Scappi, Venice, 1570, Elisha Whittelsey Collection, 52.595.2. Scappi was Pius V's chef for many years.

ON THE COVER: *The Pastry Cook*, by Abraham Bosse (French, 1602–1676), engraving, Harris Brisbane Dick Fund, 26.49.61

Copyright © 1973 by The Metropolitan Museum of Art

LIBRARY OF CONGRESS CATALOGING IN PUBLICATION DATA

Gillies, Linda, comp.
  A culinary collection.

  Half-title: A culinary collection from the Metropolitan Museum of Art.
  1. Cookery, International. I. Muller, Anita, joint comp. II. Patterson, Pamela, joint comp. III. Title.

TX725.A1G38   641.5   73–12986

ISBN 0–87099–081–0

It is a little-known and indisputable fact that museum people devote a great deal of thought and time to food, and the fare at the tables of colleagues is more often than not of the highest quality. We hope that you will enjoy this collection of recipes from members of the Board of Trustees and Staff of the Metropolitan—the Museum's first venture into the culinary aspect of the arts.

THOMAS HOVING

pignatta grande

Contents

Overheard in the Department of Drawings of the Metropolitan Museum not long ago (Secretary-Assistant to Assistant Curator): "Take one huge potato...." The exchange of recipes or views about a new cookbook or restaurant is not unusual at the Museum. After years of being a party to these conversations, we thought it might be worthwhile to collect recipes for a book, and we sent out a memorandum to the Trustees and Staff requesting them.

The response was even better than we had hoped. Recipes of all kinds came pouring in, and the result is a wonderful, international hodgepodge—something for almost every palate and schedule. American, French, Greek, Hungarian, Italian, Chinese, Korean—the cooking of twenty countries is represented. Some of the recipes involve a great deal of time (*Spiced Beef* marinates for twenty-one days!), others almost none at all (a five-minute corn purée). Some are intended for the fanciest dinners, others for at home with the kids. While the recipes divide themselves quite evenly among the various categories, the collection is uneven in parts. There are three good recipes for cheese cake, for instance, and none for other dishes that one might expect to find.

Almost every recipe has been tested; to the best of our knowledge and with a little bit of luck, they work. In the few cases in which we have left a procedure unexplained (such as, "Prepare a pie crust"), we assume that the reader will refer to one of the standard cookbooks.

Our heartiest thanks to all who helped with testing recipes: Edith Cullen, Johanna Hecht, Cynthia Lambros, and Robie Rogge.

Thanks also go to the many people who have been involved with the editing and production of the cookbook. Judith Jones, editor at Alfred A. Knopf, read the manuscript and gave us invaluable advice. Mildred Owen did a heroic job of copy-editing and lent her much needed professional touch, and Margot Feely of the Museum's Production Office handled with impeccable efficiency all aspects of the book's production. The members of the staff of the Print Department have kept the artistic side of the book in mind and set aside material to be used as illustrations, and William Pons photographed the Scappi cookbook. Peter Oldenburg adapted his innumerable talents as a designer of art books to this new sort of publication. And finally, Bradford Kelleher, Publisher at the Museum, a supporter and promoter of the project from the beginning, has been an enthusiastic source of encouragement and assistance.

Above all, we would like to thank the contributors (and their wives, husbands, friends, and staffs) who have taken the time and trouble to send in their recipes—it is they, of course, who have made the book possible.

LINDA GILLIES
ANITA MULLER
PAMELA PATTERSON

Appetizers & Soups

Cucina fetta a Campana

Martinello da fiumo

fogone alto

rota

Ipedo da ruota

Sliced Beef and Mayonnaise—
An Hors d'Oeuvre

ASHTON HAWKINS
Secretary

Carolyn and Brooke Alexander, almost as well known for their cooking as for their print gallery in New York, gave me this recipe. It is an excellent first course. An experienced and good-natured butcher is essential—the slices of beef must be paper-thin, like prosciutto.

> Approximately 1 cup mayonnaise (homemade or bottled)
> Dijon mustard
> A touch of olive oil
> Salt and pepper
> 1 pound top round beef, sliced as thinly as possible
> Chopped parsley
> Lemon wedges

Combine the mayonnaise, mustard to taste, olive oil (enough to slightly thin the mayonnaise), and salt and pepper to taste, and refrigerate. Arrange the slices of meat in one layer on plates. It is best to do this just before serving, as the meat will dry out and turn brown if left exposed to air for any length of time. If done in advance, wrap each plate tightly with plastic wrap and refrigerate. Lace each serving of meat with two or three strips of the sauce, sprinkle with parsley, and serve with a lemon wedge.

Serves 6

forcina

Salmon Roe and Radish

JOHN WALSH, JR.
European Paintings

This hors d'oeuvre is called *ikuraoroshi* in Japan. It has a distinctive, slightly astringent taste.

> 12–18 white radishes per serving
> Salmon roe ("red caviar")

Put the radishes through a meat grinder, using a fine disk. Chill. Divide into shallow bowls and make a depression in each lump of radish with a spoon. Fill with approximately 1 tablespoon of salmon roe.

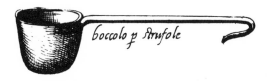

boccolo p strufole

Stuffed Smoked Salmon

MRS. VINCENT ASTOR
Trustee

A first course—good and very easy to make.

> 4 slices smoked salmon
> 1 jar potted shrimp
> 1 cup (½ pint) sour cream
> 1–2 tablespoons horseradish
> Salt and freshly ground pepper

Place a generous tablespoon of shrimp on each piece of salmon and roll up the slices. Combine the sour cream and horseradish, season to taste, and serve this sauce with the salmon.

Serves 4

Hot Crab Meat for Twenty

ELIZABETH FLINN
Junior Museum

Invariably a success at cocktail parties.

> 3 packages (8 ounces each) cream cheese, softened
> ½ cup mayonnaise
> 2 teaspoons dry mustard
> Good dash garlic salt
> ⅔ cup dry white wine
> 2 teaspoons confectioner's sugar
> 1 teaspoon onion juice
> 3 cans (6 ounces each) crab meat, drained

Combine all ingredients except crab meat and beat well. Mix in crab meat and heat thoroughly in double boiler. Serve hot on crackers or toast. May be frozen and reheated.

Serves 20

Shad Roe on Toast

FRANCIS T. P. PLIMPTON
Trustee

Mrs. Plimpton writes, "We often used this at parties when Mr. Plimpton was Deputy Representative to the U.N. It made a great hit, as shad roe is very American, not found in any other country. Serve on hot toast as a first course, on small toast circles with cocktails."

> 1 can shad roe
> ½ cup heavy cream
> A little lemon juice
> Salt and pepper
> Dash Worcestershire sauce
> 1 egg, well beaten

Heat the shad roe in a double boiler and add the cream, lemon juice, salt and pepper to taste, and Worcestershire sauce. Stir well. Just before removing from heat stir in the egg.

Serves 2 as a first course, 6 as a canapé

Canapé Seviche

HERBERT BROWNELL
General Counsel to the Museum

When Mr. Brownell was Attorney General for the United States, he and Mrs. Brownell visited Presidente and Señora Remón in Panama. At a cocktail party Señora Remón served this unusual canapé in a large bowl, surrounded by small pastry shells. It also may be a first course on lettuce with an appropriate biscuit. In Panama seviche is made from corbina fish; because it is firm, sea bass is the best substitute here.

> Sea bass or flounder, cut into tiny cubes
> Lime juice
> Dash of hot red pepper
> Finely chopped onion
> Olive oil
> Salt (optional)
> Tomato juice (optional)

Combine all ingredients (the amounts depend on your taste and the number of persons to be served). Cover, and marinate at room temperature for 6 to 8 hours. The lime juice "cooks" the fish. Store in the refrigerator until time to serve.

navicella alta

Mousse Romsey

JOAN GOULD
Bulletin and Calendar/News

We first had this at a summer supper in the charming little English town of Romsey, near Southampton.

> 1 can (4 ½ ounces) little shrimp
> 6 ounces cream cheese
> 1 can jellied consommé or madrilène
> 1 tablespoon sherry or madeira
> Parsley or tarragon

Cover the bottoms of four small ramekins with shrimp. Mix cream cheese, about seven-eighths of the consommé or madrilène, and wine in blender. Pour mixture into ramekins, almost to top. Chill, and when firm cover top of each ramekin with remaining consommé or madrilène. Chill again, until top layer is jelled. Before serving decorate with parsley or tarragon. Can easily be done the night before.

Serves 4

Cold Tomato Cobb

HERBERT BROWNELL
General Counsel to the Museum

Mrs. Brownell contributed this recipe. "I love giving recipes," she said. "Someday I'll write my own cookbook."

> 5 tablespoons mayonnaise
> 1 heaping tablespoon minced parsley
> 1 teaspoon curry powder
> 7 large ripe tomatoes, peeled, seeded, and cut into small, firm pieces
> 1 small white onion, grated
> 1½ teaspoons salt
> ¼ teaspoon pepper

Combine the mayonnaise, parsley, and curry powder, and refrigerate. When cold, mix in the tomatoes, onion, and seasonings. Pour into a freezing tray and freeze until slightly frozen. Serve in bouillon cups or small bowls.

Serves 4

Avocado Yogurt Dip Olé

FRANCES KAPLAN
Sales

A variation on guacamole.

> 1 large avocado, mashed
> 3 tablespoons lemon juice
> Garlic powder
> Salt
> 1½ cups plain yogurt
> Onion soup mix

Mix the avocado, lemon juice, and garlic powder and salt to taste. Combine the yogurt with as much of the onion soup mix as suits you. Add the avocado mixture and beat until smooth. If a thinner consistency is wanted, add a little more yogurt.

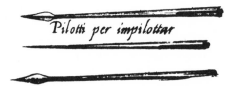

Piloti per impilottar

Near Eastern Chickpea Dip

ELIZABETH FLINN
Junior Museum

Serve with Arabic bread or crackers.

> 1 can (1 pound, 4 ounces) chickpeas
> ⅓ cup olive oil
> ½ cup finely chopped onion
> 1 teaspoon salt
> 2 tablespoons lemon juice
> ¼ teaspoon pepper
> ⅓ cup chopped black olives
> ½ cup sour cream (optional)

Place all ingredients except sour cream in blender and blend until mixture is smooth. Stir in sour cream, if desired.

Liptauer

PETER FISCHER
Carpenter's Shop

To be spread on rye or pumpernickel as canapés; also a good base for cold-cut sandwiches. A teaspoon of chopped fresh chives or dried onion is a good but not a very authentic addition.

> 4 ounces cream cheese, at room temperature
> ¼ pound sweet butter, at room temperature
> 1 small sour pickle, finely chopped
> 1 tablespoon capers, finely chopped
> 1 tablespoon anchovy paste (or 4 fillets, chopped)
> 1 teaspoon Hungarian paprika
> 1 teaspoon finely grated sapsago cheese (optional)

Mix all ingredients with a fork in a small bowl. If doubling or tripling the recipe, one can use an electric mixer.

Roquefort Cheese Ball

EDITH CULLEN
Drawings

Something different for cocktails.

> 1 pound Roquefort cheese (more if needed)
> ½ cup butter
> Dash Worcestershire sauce
> Dash Tabasco
> 2 tablespoons minced celery
> 2 tablespoons minced onion
> ½ tablespoon finely chopped parsley
> 1 teaspoon chili powder
> 1 teaspoon salt
> 1 teaspoon pepper
> 4–5 tablespoons cognac
> Finely ground bread crumbs (if needed)
> 1 cup ground walnuts

Mash cheese in a bowl with a fork. Add butter and mix until creamy. Add all other ingredients except bread crumbs and walnuts. Use electric mixer at medium to high speed to fluff mixture. If mixture is too moist, add more cheese or some finely ground bread crumbs. Place in refrigerator overnight (or for several days). Work into one large ball or several small ones on waxed paper. Roll in ground walnuts.

Orange and Cream Cheese Canapés

LORETTA HOWARD
Western European Arts

Mrs. Howard, a well-known collector of crèche figures, decorates the Metropolitan's Christmas tree each year with Neapolitan figures that she has given to the Museum. Appropriately, her canapés might be served at a holiday party.

> Cream cheese, at room temperature
> Orange or lemon juice
> Onion juice
> Salt and pepper
> Small rounds of bread sautéed in butter
> Grated orange rind

Soften the cream cheese with a little fruit juice and then add onion juice and seasonings to taste. Spread onto bread rounds and sprinkle with orange rind. Serve cold.

Fairly Simple Dip

NANCY RUSSELL
Library

The recipe that has brought me the most consistent raves is one I adapted to accommodate various allergies. Mix, scoop, and swoon.

> 1 cup (½ pint) sour cream
> 1 cup coarsely grated sharp cheddar cheese
> ½–1 teaspoon prepared mustard (the yellowest kind gives the pleasantest color)
> 1 tablespoon chopped parsley
> Some form of onion flavoring: chopped chives or onion powder (optional)

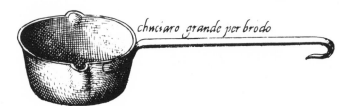

Pamela McVeigh's Grandmother's Chef's Vichyssoise

LINDA GILLIES
Drawings

From a former assistant in the Drawings Department. Less rich than most recipes of this kind, as one does not use cream.

> 1 huge potato, chopped
> 1 huge Bermuda onion, chopped
> ¼ pound butter
> ¼ cup white wine
> 1 tablespoon lemon juice
> 2–3 chicken bouillon cubes

Put all ingredients in a pot with water to cover. Cook until the potatoes and onions are tender, then put through a blender. Chill.

Serves 4

Cold Cucumber Soup

MARISE JOHNSON
Far Eastern Art

Easy and useful.

> 1 cucumber, peeled, seeded, and diced
> 1½ cups buttermilk
> 1 tablespoon lime juice
> 2 cups chicken broth
> ¼ teaspoon lemon pepper
> Dash curry (optional)
> Finely chopped chives

Place all ingredients except chives in blender and blend until fairly smooth. Chill well and serve sprinkled with chives. If the soup separates, return to blender for several seconds.

Serves 6

Andalusian Gazpacho

CARMEN GOMEZ-MORENO
Medieval Art

The gazpacho, which is now internationally known, used to be a regional summer soup that was not considered elegant among the all-time snobs. The one best known out of Andalusia originates in Seville and, thanks to the blender, has become very simple and fast to make. Enjoy its cooling delight on a hot summer day.

> SOUP 2 pieces stale bread, crusts removed
> 3 tablespoons vinegar
> 3 or 4 very red, ripe tomatoes, peeled, or one
>   16-ounce can plum tomatoes
> 1 or 2 pieces of cucumber peel (optional)
> 1 or 2 cloves garlic
> 2 tablespoons olive oil
> Salt and pepper
> 1 quart water and/or tomato juice

ACCOMPA-
NIMENTS
2 cucumbers, peeled and diced
2 green peppers, diced
2 tomatoes, diced
Bread crust, broken into small pieces with the
fingers

In a small bowl soak the bread with 1 tablespoon of the vinegar and 1 tablespoon water. Put it in a blender with the tomatoes, cucumber peel if wished, garlic, oil, and remaining vinegar. Blend the mixture at high speed for 1 minute—it is best if not too smooth. Season to taste. If it is not to be served immediately, refrigerate (the soup improves if chilled for several hours or overnight). Before serving add water to taste. If the tomatoes are not very tasty, mix tomato juice with the water. Serve in chilled bowls accompanied by the diced vegetables and bread in individual dishes. Let the guests help themselves, since not everybody likes everything—some want bread, some hate cucumber or green pepper; some prefer to have it as it is.

Serves 4

Mario's Gazpacho

CHEF MARIO
Restaurant

Although the Metropolitan's chef comes from northern Italy and claims to have received his most valuable training while working at Lüchow's in New York, a restaurant specializing in German food, he seems to have captured the secret to the Spanish gazpacho.

SOUP
1 clove garlic, peeled and chopped
1 medium onion, chopped
1 cucumber, peeled and chopped
3 tomatoes, peeled and chopped
1 green pepper, chopped
2 eggs
¼ cup wine vinegar
¾ cup V-8 or tomato juice
⅛ teaspoon salt
⅛ teaspoon cayenne pepper
2 sprigs fresh tarragon (optional)
¼ cup olive oil

ACCOMPA-
NIMENTS
Cucumber cubes
Chopped onion
Chopped green pepper
Croutons sautéed in garlic and oil

Place all soup ingredients except olive oil in a blender, and blend for 10 seconds. Strain and chill. Stir in olive oil and mix well; add more tomato juice if it seems necessary. Serve cucumber, onion, green pepper, and croutons in separate bowls.

Serves 6

Cold Tomato Soup

INGE HECKEL
Development and Promotion

A variation on gazpacho.

7 very large, ripe tomatoes, peeled, or 1 can
   (35 ounces) whole tomatoes, with juice
1 small white onion, chopped
1½ teaspoons salt
¼ teaspoon pepper
5 tablespoons mayonnaise
1 teaspoon minced parsley
1 teaspoon curry powder

Place tomatoes, onion, salt, and pepper in a blender, and mix until smooth. Transfer mixture to a bowl, and beat in remaining ingredients with a wire whisk until smooth and creamy. Serve very cold in chilled soup cups.

Serves 4

Kathy's Spinach Soup

LINDA GILLIES
Drawings

A rich soup that is also good and very pretty served cold and sprinkled with grated egg yolk and blanched, slivered lemon rind.

> 4 tablespoons butter
> 2 tablespoons flour
> 2 cups milk
> 1 cup light cream
> 1 cup cooked chopped spinach, well drained
> 1 bouillon cube
> 1½ tablespoons sherry
> 1 small onion, studded with two whole cloves
> Salt, pepper, nutmeg

Put butter, flour, 1 cup of the milk, cream, and spinach in blender for 5 seconds. Place mixture in top of double boiler, heat over flame quickly, and add bouillon cube and most of remaining milk. Stir over hot water until creamy. Add sherry and onion, and simmer for 10 minutes. If it seems too thick, add a little more milk. Season with salt, pepper, and nutmeg. Remove onion and serve.

Serves 4

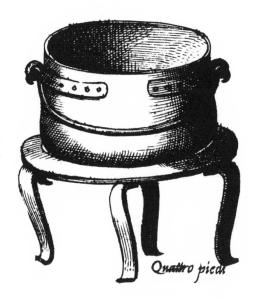

Quattro piedi

Fresh Vegetable Soup

CLARE VINCENT
Western European Arts

The secret to this recipe is adding the vegetables to the pot in the right order. If done properly, the time needed to peel and chop each variety of vegetable will just about match the time required by each for cooking.

2 leeks, cut in ½-inch chunks

1 medium or large onion, cut in ½-inch chunks

2 tablespoons butter

6 chicken bouillon cubes

2 parsnips, cut in ½-inch chunks

2 medium white turnips, cut in ½-inch chunks

2–3 stalks celery (without leaves), cut in ½-inch chunks

2 medium carrots, cut in thumb-size pieces

¼ teaspoon dried thyme (or more)

¼ teaspoon dried rosemary (or more)

Salt and freshly ground pepper

2 medium potatoes, cut in thumb-size pieces

2 cups stewed tomatoes (one 16-ounce can), crushed

3 tablespoons chopped fresh parsley

3 tablespoons chopped fresh dill

In a large pot wilt leeks and onions in butter. Add 3 quarts of water and bouillon cubes and bring to a boil. Add parsnips and bring to a boil. Add turnips and bring to a boil. Add celery and bring to a boil. Add carrots and bring to a boil. Add thyme, rosemary, salt, and pepper, and correct seasoning (more herbs and bouillon may be added). Add potatoes and bring to a boil. Add tomatoes, bring to a boil, and simmer until potatoes are nearly cooked through. All the other vegetables will be ready by this time. Add parsley and dill, and simmer until the potatoes are done and the herbs have just begun to wilt.

When reheating to serve, make sure not to allow soup to simmer more than a minute or two, or all the care in bringing each vegetable to just the right degree of doneness will be wasted.

Serves 8

Cream of Vegetable Soup

HENRY GELDZAHLER
Twentieth-Century Art

One of the simplest soups imaginable. Yet its richness and delicacy make it a fitting first course, no matter how "haute" the cuisine that follows. Quantities depend on the ingredients you happen to have and how much you need. Thanks for this recipe and Three Ways to Cook Brown Rice (page 106) go to Christopher Scott.

> Leftover pressure-cooked rice
> Any vegetable or combination of vegetables:
>   thinly sliced cabbage, onions, carrots, turnips,
>   radishes
> Salt
> Soy sauce (optional)

Cook the rice with water, covered, until it becomes a porridge. Put through a food mill, reserving the bran left in the mill for home-made bread, crackers, or *beignets*. Dilute porridge to soup consistency, bring to a boil, and add vegetables. Cook gently from 15 minutes to 1 hour, depending on the vegetables. Season to taste and cook an additional 5 minutes. In the winter add soy sauce for a hearty beef flavor.

Lobster Stew

DOUGLAS DILLON
Trustee

The secret is to allow the soup to stand for a day before serving.

> 2 chicken lobsters (½ lobster per serving or bowl)
> ¼ pound butter
> 1½ pints light cream
> ½ pint heavy cream
> Salt and freshly ground pepper

Put live lobsters into a large pot of boiling water and boil for 15 minutes; remove meat immediately and cut into fairly large pieces. Melt the butter in a large skillet, add the lobster, and stir for 8 minutes over low heat. Cool slightly and very slowly add the light and heavy cream, still stirring. Reheat, but do not boil. Add salt and pepper to taste. Refrigerate for 24 hours. Reheat over low heat, stirring constantly. Do not boil.

Serves 4

Jean's Crab Soup

LINDA GILLIES
Drawings

The answer to a prayer for the hurried cook, as this tastes and looks much fancier than its canned ingredients suggest.

> 1 can tomato soup
> 1 can pea soup
> 1 can beef consommé
> Pinch pepper
> Dash mace
> ½ cup light cream
> 1 tablespoon sherry
> ¼ pound crab meat

Mix the soups, pepper, and mace. Heat until very hot. At the last minute add the cream and sherry. Heat soup bowls and place one heaping tablespoon of crab meat in the center of each one. Slowly pour the soup into the bowls and serve immediately.

Serves 4

Fish Soup

JAMES J. RORIMER
(1905–1966)

Mr. Rorimer, Director of the Museum from 1955 until his death, was a passionate cook. Mrs. Rorimer sent us this recipe and Sunday Night Menu (page 162), favorites of his. The soup is adaptable to one's imagination and to the ingredients one's neighborhood has to offer. The heavy iron or glazed pottery vessel with a tight lid is important.

1 medium clove garlic, minced
1 medium onion, chopped
2 tablespoons butter
Salt and pepper or paprika
1 tomato, chopped
1 pound shrimp, cleaned
¾ pound halibut, boned
3 squid, bones and eyes removed, sliced
5 lobster tails (or other shellfish)
18 clams, scrubbed
Bay leaves
Chopped parsley

In a large heavy iron or glazed pottery pot sauté the garlic and onion in butter; when almost tender add the tomato and cook for a few minutes longer, being careful that the garlic and onion do not brown. Stir in salt and pepper or paprika to taste. Arrange the seafood on top of the vegetables, the clams last. Cover the seafood, except for the clams, with boiling water. Add the bay leaves and parsley. Cover and boil gently, over asbestos if possible, for 30 minutes, when the clams should have opened (discard any unopened clams). Sprinkle with more parsley and serve immediately.

Serves 5

Quick Fish Soup

PAMELA PATTERSON
Sales

Making a fish soup in a large plastic oven bag is an alarming prospect, but it *works* (the bag does not leak!). The fish is tender and the broth rich—good served with garlic bread.

2 tablespoons flour
1 oven-roasting bag, largest size available
3 pounds firm white fish (cusk or scrod)
16 clams, scrubbed
16 mussels, scrubbed and debearded
1 pound shrimp, cleaned
3 hard-shell crabs or 1 small lobster, cut up
1 can (10 ½ ounces) white clam sauce
1 can (16 ounces) tomatoes
1 large onion, minced
2–3 cloves garlic, minced
2–3 dashes Tabasco
Salt and pepper
4–6 cups liquid (white wine, clam juice, water, or
   a combination)
Chopped parsley

pignatta

Preheat oven to 375°.

Shake flour in oven-roasting bag. (If bag appears too small, divide ingredients and cook in two bags.) Lay bag on its side and place white fish in it. Surround with remaining ingredients, except parsley, tipping the edges of the bag up so that the liquid will not run out. The bag should be approximately two-thirds full. Pierce the top 4 to 6 times (very important—otherwise it will explode). Place in a roasting pan and bake 30 to 45 minutes, or until clams and mussels have been open 5 minutes. Pour into tureen and sprinkle with parsley. Will remain hot and perfect in sealed bag with oven turned off for about 30 minutes.

Serves 6

Soup "Al Cuarto de Hora"

CARMEN GOMEZ-MORENO
Medieval Art

Its name indicates that this soup can be made in just 15 minutes.

18 clams
2 tablespoons olive oil
2 tablespoons minced onion
4 slices ham, diced
3 ripe tomatoes, peeled, seeded, and chopped
8 cups liquid (a combination of the broth in which
    the clams were cooked, additional bottled clam
    juice, white wine, and water—to taste)
6 ounces haddock, cut in small pieces
1 haddock or other fish head (gives a stronger fish
    flavor—optional)
½ pound shrimp, cleaned
½ cup frozen green peas
2 tablespoons raw rice
1 sprig parsley
Paprika or Spanish red pepper (optional)
Salt and freshly ground pepper
6 slices bread, crusts removed
Butter
1 hard-boiled egg, finely chopped

Cover the clams with water and cook until they open. Remove clams from their shells and set aside, reserving the broth. Heat the oil in a large casserole and add the onion and ham. Cover and cook very slowly until the onion is transparent. Add the tomatoes and cook for 5 minutes. Add the liquid of your choice, fish, fish head if wished, shrimp, peas, rice, parsley, paprika or red pepper, and salt and pepper to taste, and boil gently for 15 minutes, or until rice is tender. In the meantime, fry the bread in butter and keep warm. Remove the fish head if you have used one, add the clams and egg, and pour the soup into a tureen over the slices of fried bread.

Serves 6

Bone Soup

MARY RUSSEL
Sales

Once I had only 21 cents to create my evening meal. Feeling poor and discouraged, even so I went to my corner supermarket to see if anything could be had for that amount. There suddenly in the great case was a packet of bones marked exactly 21 cents. "Voilà! That's it!" cried I and went home to make such a delicious soup that any inclination to feel depressed about my own pocket of poverty—my studio life as an artist who never sells a painting— vanished. Bones provide a satisfying base for a meal, and as for the other ingredients, the point of poverty cooking is to use whatever you happen to have.

> 1 pound lamb, veal, or beef bones (choose the ones
>   with the most meat, avoiding fat and sinews)
> Salt and pepper
> Herbs: oregano, basil, rosemary, bay leaf, parsley
> 1 cup dried peas, lentils, or rice, or a combination
> Fresh vegetables: onions, carrots, celery tops

Cover the bones with water and add seasoning and herbs to taste. Bring to a boil, and simmer, covered, for up to an hour. Add the peas or lentils or rice and simmer for 45 minutes. Add the vegetables and cook, still covered, for another 30 minutes. The meat should be very tender, falling off the bones. The marrow will be delicious, too.

Serves 2

Caldaro da 4 Jome

Korean Spinach Soup

ANITA KOH
Ancient Near Eastern Art

Along with rice and kimchi, a hearty soup is almost always part of a Korean meal. You can substitute other vegetables such as bean sprouts or seaweed. Use your imagination.

1–2 tablespoons sesame oil
¼ pound sirloin tip, cut into very thin strips
1–2 cloves garlic
2 tablespoons soy sauce
1 tablespoon toasted sesame seeds
½ pound spinach, washed and drained
Salt
2 scallions, chopped

Heat the oil in a large pot, add meat and garlic, and sear. Mix in soy sauce, 7 cups water and the sesame seeds, bring to a boil, and simmer 10 to 15 minutes. Salt to taste. Add the spinach and cook for 2 to 5 minutes. Add the scallions 1 minute before the soup is done.

Serves 6

Caldaro

Lentil Soup à la Edison
(a new invention every time)

VIRGINIA BURTON
Egyptian Art

This soup was invented by the late Albert TenEyck Gardner, formerly Curator of American Paintings. "A rich solid soup you can lean on," he wrote. "By varying the amounts of seasonings or experimenting with things not on my list *you* can be an inventor."

BASIC INGREDIENTS	1 pound lentils, washed in cold water
	3–4 teaspoons salt
	½ cup vegetable oil
	2 medium onions, quartered
	4–6 stalks celery with leaves
	2–3 cloves garlic, minced or sliced
	1–2 cups wine (preferably dry madeira or vermouth, but red or white wine or even sherry will do)
	1–2 cups beef or chicken stock
OPTIONAL	Chicken, beef, ham, or any meat leftovers
	Carrots, peas, tomatoes, beans, or any other vegetables you find in the refrigerator
	1 cup chopped mushrooms
	1 lemon, quartered
	6–8 peppercorns
	Freshly ground pepper
	Marjoram
	2–3 bay leaves
	Celery seeds or flakes
	2 tablespoons honey or jelly
	Paprika
	Shredded coconut (terribly exotic)
	2–3 dashes Tabasco sauce

In 3 quarts of water bring to a boil all the basic ingredients and any of the optional ones you choose to include. Simmer until the lentils are tender, about 2 hours. Remove celery and bay leaves, and correct seasoning. Refrigerate (it will keep for about a week, longer if there is no meat) or freeze.

Serves 8 (about 2 quarts)

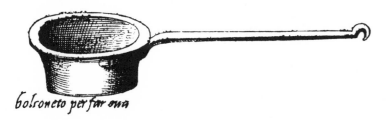

bolroneto per far ova

Borscht

LINDA GILLIES
Drawings

This recipe is from a member of the Visiting Committee to the Drawings Department, Gregoire Tarnopol. More of a stew than a soup, the borscht is perfect for a Sunday night supper. Serve it with crusty bread and red or white wine, followed by chocolate mousse.

2 pounds beef chuck, cut as if for stew

2–3 soup bones (veal, if possible)

1 medium-size onion, roughly chopped

1 tablespoon salt

1 teaspoon pepper

5 fresh tomatoes, peeled and seeded, or 1 large can stewed tomatoes, drained

4 fresh beets, peeled and sliced, or 1 medium can sliced beets

1 bay leaf

1 cabbage, coarsely shredded

3–4 potatoes (depending on size), peeled and quartered

Juice from 3 lemons

Sugar

2 tablespoons finely chopped fresh dill

Place meat, bones, onion, salt, and pepper in a large, heavy pot and add water barely to cover. Bring to a boil and skim fat from surface. Add tomatoes, beets, and bay leaf, and simmer, partially covered, for 2 hours. Add cabbage, potatoes, and lemon juice, and cook, partially covered, for another 45 minutes. Add sugar to taste. Cool, remove bones, and refrigerate overnight. Before serving remove fat that has congealed on surface, reheat slowly, correct seasoning, and sprinkle with dill.

Serves 4

concha

Hungarian Party Soup

MARICA VILCEK
Catalogue

In Hungary this pungent, delicious soup is often served toward the end of a late evening party, such as New Year's Eve. It can be prepared well in advance and slowly reheated.

1 pound sauerkraut, well washed and drained

1 ham hock, if available, or 2 pieces of knackwurst

½ teaspoon peppercorns

1 bay leaf

1½ – 2 ounces dried mushrooms (not fresh ones),
   washed and drained

1 large onion, chopped

2 tablespoons butter

4 tablespoons flour

1 teaspoon Hungarian sweet paprika

1 teaspoon caraway seeds

1 pound Polish (kielbasa) or sweet Spanish
   (chorizo) sausage, sliced into ½-inch pieces

1 cup sour cream

Salt

Vinegar (optional)

Simmer the sauerkraut, ham bone or knackwurst, peppercorns, bay leaf, and mushrooms with 4 cups of water in a large pot, covered, for 1 hour. In a skillet sauté chopped onions in butter until transparent. Stir in flour and cook over low heat for about 2 minutes (do not allow roux to color). Off the heat add the paprika and caraway seeds, mix until smooth, return to low heat, and cook for 1 minute. Dilute the roux by stirring in boiling stock from the sauerkraut. When the roux is smooth and not too thick, stir it into the boiling soup. Add sausage slices and boil gently, uncovered, for an additional 15 minutes. Remove ham bone (or knackwurst) and skim off excess fat. Add the sour cream, mix well, and add salt to taste. Add vinegar if it seems necessary, but with caution. Reheat slowly before serving.

Serves 6

Meats, Poultry, Fish, & Their Sauces

Holiday Spiced Beef

LEWIS SHARP
*American Paintings and
Sculpture*

Sandwiches made of this spiced beef and hot mustard have been a traditional Sharp Christmas Eve supper for several generations. The meat lasts for snacks all during the holidays. A prerequisite for the recipe is a big house with a cold storage room, where the beef can marinate for 21 days.

1 pound salt
1 pound brown sugar
¼ ounce saltpeter
½ ounce ground cloves
½ ounce ground cinnamon
½ ounce allspice
1 nutmeg, grated
20 pounds top round beef (have the butcher cut
    into the center of the meat and tie it tightly
    around an 8-inch length of big bone)

Mix all the dry ingredients and rub well into the meat. Place in a crock and rub and turn every day for 21 days. The meat will make its own brine. Wash well. Cover with water, bring to a boil, and cook slowly for 4 hours. Let the meat stand in the same water overnight. Remove from water and refrigerate.

Serves 50

Boiled Beef with Salsa Verde

PHYLLIS DEARBORN MASSAR
Prints and Photographs

For a true Italian bollito, chicken, veal, and cotechino sausage may all be boiled along with the shin and served on the same platter, along with young carrots, string beans, boiled potatoes, or any other vegetable. Guests select what they prefer. The salsa verde is passed in a bowl.

MEAT
1 beef shin, cut in 1-inch pieces
1 carrot, sliced
1 small onion, sliced
1 stalk celery (with leaves), chopped
1 bay leaf
5 peppercorns
Salt

SAUCE
¾ cup finely chopped parsley
½ cup olive oil
¼ cup vinegar
1 or 2 cloves garlic, minced
Salt and pepper
Capers (if you like them)
1 anchovy, mashed (if you wish)

Meat. Rinse the meat, place it in a deep kettle with the vegetables, bay leaf, peppercorns, and salt, and cover with water. Bring to a boil, skimming as often as necessary to remove the scum. Simmer, partially covered, for 3 hours. Skim the fat. Or better, cool and refrigerate overnight; then remove the solidified fat. Reheat in the broth (which, strained, makes a lovely base for soup; or add small pasta to it and serve as is), slice, and arrange on a platter.

Sauce. Combine all the ingredients and let them ripen in the refrigerator for a day or two. Shake well before serving.

Serves 4

Le Sauerbraten

MARICA VILCEK
Catalogue

A sumptuous version of one of the staples of Central European cooking. Plan ahead—it takes several days' preparation. Serve with dumplings, spaetzle, nockerl, gnocchi, or quenelles. Lingonberries or cranberry sauce can also accompany sauerbraten.

MEAT
- A 5-pound piece of beef (preferably rump, but top or bottom round, chuck, or eye round will do)
- 5 slices of bacon, pork fat, or salt pork, cut into ¼-inch lardons and sprinkled with brandy and black pepper
- Salt and pepper
- 3–4 tablespoons vegetable oil

MARINADE
- 3 tablespoons butter
- 3 tablespoons cooking oil
- 2 cups coarsely chopped onions
- 2 cups sliced carrots
- 1½ cups diced celery root (or celery)
- 1½ cups diced parsley roots (or 10 sprigs parsley, coarsely chopped)
- 1–2 leeks, sliced
- ⅓ cup brandy
- Rind of 1 lemon, chopped
- Juice of 2 lemons
- 4 tablespoons vinegar
- 3 cups red wine
- 2 cups beef broth
- 10–15 peppercorns
- 3–4 whole cloves
- 3–4 allspice berries
- 6–8 juniper berries
- 3 bay leaves
- 2 cardamom seeds
- 1 teaspoon dried crushed thyme
- ½ teaspoon dried crushed red pepper
- ½ teaspoon fennel seeds
- ½ teaspoon mustard seeds

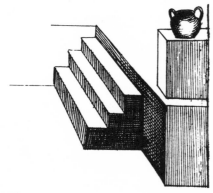

Cucumio

SAUCE   ⅓ cup dry sherry or dry vermouth

1 teaspoon meat glaze

1–2 teaspoons Dijon mustard

1 tablespoon red currant jelly

1–2 cups beef broth (if necessary)

1–2 tablespoons cornstarch or potato starch,
dissolved in ¼ cup broth or water (if necessary)

2 cups sour cream

Salt, pepper, red cayenne, lemon juice, or vinegar
(if necessary)

Larding the meat. For best results, the meat should be larded with fat. (Some butchers will do the larding for you.) This process lends flavor, keeps the meat from drying out, tenderizes it, and keeps it from shrinking. Punch holes into the meat about 1 inch apart and with a larding needle or thin pointed knife insert the lardons. If a less porky flavor is wanted, blanch the lardons briefly first. Rub the meat with salt and pepper and tie with a string. Place in an enamel, glass, or porcelain (not metal) bowl.

Marinade. In a large casserole heat the butter and oil, add the onions, and cook until transparent. Gradually add the other vegetables and cook until light brown. Add the brandy, lemon rind and juice, vinegar, wine, and broth. Tie the spices up in cheesecloth and add them. Bring to a boil and simmer for 1 or 2 minutes. Cool and pour over meat. The marinade should cover the meat. Marinate in the refrigerator for at least 2 days, turning frequently.

Cooking the meat. Preheat oven to 350°. Remove the meat from the marinade and dry it carefully. Let stand at room temperature for 1 to 2 hours. Heat the vegetable oil in a heavy enamel casserole and brown the meat on all sides over a high heat. Remove the meat and pour off cooking oil. Return the meat to the pan, add 1½ cups of the marinade liquid, cover tightly, and bring to a simmer on top of the stove. Transfer to oven and roast, basting frequently, for 1½ hours. Add the remaining marinade (with vegetables) and roast for an additional 1 to 1½ hours, or until meat is tender.

Sauce. Remove the cooked meat from the casserole and keep it warm. Put the marinade and vegetables through a sieve or fine food mill. If the purée is put through a blender at this point, the sauce

frofator

will be particularly smooth. Return the purée to the casserole, bring to a boil, and add the wine, meat glaze, mustard, and jelly. The sauce should have the consistency of a rather thick tomato sauce. If it is too thick, add broth; if too thin, add starch. Gradually beat in the sour cream with a wire whisk. Very carefully correct the seasoning (the sauce should have a touch of sharpness to it). Slice the meat and cover generously with sauce.

The dish may be prepared in advance; slowly bring the sauce to a simmer and warm the meat up in it.

Serves 8

Sauerbraten with Potato Balls

ARTHUR KLEIN
Plans and Construction

SAUER- BRATEN	
	2 cups cider vinegar
	2 cups water
	1 medium onion, sliced
	8 whole cloves
	4 bay leaves
	2 tablespoons salt
	1 teaspoon pepper
	2 tablespoons sugar
	4–5 pounds beef (sirloin tip or eye round)
	Flour
	2 tablespoons cooking oil
	4 tablespoons butter or margarine
	1 tablespoon sugar
	8–10 ginger snaps, crushed

Combine the first 8 ingredients to make marinade. Place meat in a large, deep nonmetallic bowl and pour marinade over it. Cover and refrigerate for 36 to 48 hours, turning meat once or twice a day. Remove meat and pat dry. Rub lightly with a little flour. Heat oil and 1 tablespoon of butter or margarine, and brown meat well on all sides. Strain the marinade and add 2 cups to the meat. Cover and

42

simmer for 3 hours. Melt remaining 3 tablespoons of butter or margarine, blend in 6 tablespoons of flour and the sugar, and stir until the mixture is a rich brown. Add the remaining strained marinade, stir until smooth, and pour into the sauce simmering with the meat. Simmer 1 hour longer, or until meat is tender. Remove meat and add ginger snaps to the sauce; stir until thickened. Serve with the meat.

POTATO	8–10 medium potatoes
BALLS	½ teaspoon pepper
	2 tablespoons salt
	Flour
	2 eggs
	1 cup fine dry bread crumbs

Wash and boil the potatoes until tender. Peel, and quarter them, and put through ricer. Refrigerate until cold. Add pepper, salt, 4 tablespoons of flour, eggs, and bread crumbs to the riced potatoes. Mix thoroughly with your hands. Then flour your hands and make medium-size balls; roll each ball in flour. Place them in slowly boiling salted water, about six at a time. They will sink to the bottom and rise to the surface in about 5 to 8 minutes. Cook another 2 to 3 minutes. Drain and keep warm in the oven until all potato balls are cooked. Serve with sauerbraten.

Serves 8

padella ovata

Bulgogee

ANITA KOH
Ancient Near Eastern Art

A teriyakilike marinated beef. If you have a charcoal broiler and some way to keep the meat from falling into the fire, this is even closer to the way bulgogee is actually cooked in Korea (on a domed metal utensil over a charcoal fire).

Conserva mezana

1½ pounds sirloin tip beef, cut in paper-thin slices
    about 1 inch wide
2 tablespoons Oriental sesame oil
2 tablespoons sugar
2 scallions, chopped (including green tops)
1–2 cloves garlic, chopped
2 tablespoons toasted sesame seeds
6 tablespoons Japanese or Korean soy sauce

Mix the beef, sesame oil, and sugar. Add the remaining ingredients, and allow to sit for at least 15 minutes—the longer the better (refrigerate if it marinates overnight). Arrange meat on a rack in a broiling pan and broil until cooked through but still juicy.

Serves 4

Oxtail Stew

JAMES DELIHAS
Public Affairs

Inexpensive and very tasty, this stew improves enormously with second and third reheatings, and is best several days old. It is good served with steamed new potatoes. Other vegetables can be successfully substituted for or added to the carrots—sliced celery, diced turnips, peas, fresh or drained canned tomatoes. A couple of tablespoons of madeira can be added just before serving. If the stew is for company, supply the guests with plates for the bones.

3 pounds oxtail, cut into pieces
½ cup flour (approximately)
Salt and pepper
2 tablespoons butter
2 tablespoons oil
2 large onions, chopped
2 cans (10½ ounces each) beef consommé (not
    beef broth)
1 teaspoon marjoram or thyme
1 bay leaf
3 carrots, sliced
Chopped parsley

Trim the oxtail pieces of fat. The larger pieces are apt to have a ring of fat that should be cut away. Shake the pieces in a paper bag with the flour, salt, and pepper. Melt the butter with the oil in a large skillet, and brown the pieces well (adding more butter and oil as needed). As pieces are browned remove them to a large (4- to 5-quart) casserole. Brown the onions quickly in the same skillet and add to the casserole. Pour the consommé over the meat and add water to just cover. Add the marjoram or thyme and bay leaf, bring to a boil on top of the stove, cover, and simmer for 3½ to 4 hours, or until the meat is very tender and almost falls from the bones. Cool the stew and refrigerate overnight. Skim off the solidified fat. Heat stew slowly over a low flame until it simmers. Add the carrots, cover, and cook for 30 minutes, or until they are tender. Sprinkle with parsley and serve.

Serves 6

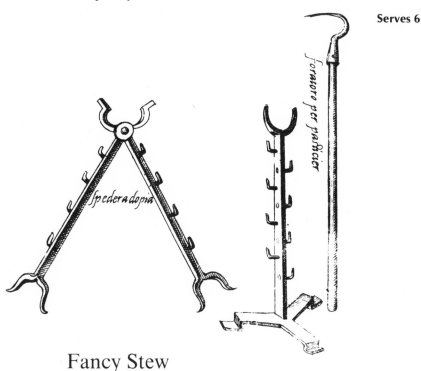

Fancy Stew

ANN LEVEN
Treasurer

Between a classic boeuf Bourguignon and an old-fashioned beef stew. It is very flexible, adaptable to your mood and larder. While dried herbs are fine, fresh ones lend a really special flavor.

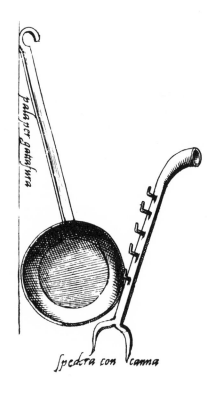

pala per gatafura

ſpedra con canna

¼ pound bacon or salt pork, minced

2 large yellow onions, sliced

2 cloves garlic, minced

2½ pounds beef chuck, cut in 1½-inch cubes

Oil (if necessary)

½ pound small white onions, peeled

¾ pound mushrooms, whole, quartered, or sliced,
    depending on size

2½ tablespoons flour

2 tablespoons tomato paste

2–3 cups (approximately) red burgundy, or half
    wine, half beef bouillon

1 bay leaf

A big sprig of whatever fresh herb you have on
    hand: tarragon, rosemary, sage, etc., or
    1 teaspoon of a dried herb

¼ cup brandy (optional)

Salt and pepper

Minced parsley

Vegetables: carrots, peas, beans (optional)

Sauté the bacon or salt pork until golden in a Dutch oven, remove pieces with a slotted spoon, and reserve. Sauté the sliced onions and garlic in the same fat until tender and set aside with bacon. Brown the beef in the same fat a few pieces at a time, adding oil if necessary, and set aside. Cook the whole onions and mushrooms in the same pan, stirring for 3 minutes, and set aside. In a small bowl mix the flour and tomato paste with a little wine or bouillon until smooth. Stir mixture into the pan, adding the remaining liquid, meat (the meat should be almost covered), herbs, and reserved bacon, yellow and white onions, garlic, and mushrooms. Simmer, covered, for 1½ hours, or until the beef is tender. Add the brandy if you wish, correct seasoning, and cook, uncovered, for 15 minutes. Sprinkle with parsley and serve. If you wish to include vegetables, add them to the stew so that they will cook for the appropriate time.

Even better if made the day before. Remove the congealed fat and slowly reheat.

Serves 4 to 6

Hungarian Goulash
(and not so Hungarian)

PETER FISCHER
Carpenter's Shop

This recipe is adaptable to any odds and ends you may have in the vegetable bin—potatoes, carrots, peas, mushrooms. Add them 30 minutes before the stew is finished cooking. Frozen vegetables may also be used, but of course should be cooked less time. Whatever the ingredients may end up being, the stew is best if made the day before serving and reheated.

2 pounds beef chuck, cut into 1-inch cubes

2 tablespoons flour

1 teaspoon salt

¼ teaspoon pepper

2–3 tablespoons peanut or other oil

2 onions, chopped or thinly sliced

¼ cup chopped fresh parsley, or 1 tablespoon dried

1 can chicken broth or any of the following:
consommé, mushroom, vegetable, or onion soup

1 can (16 ounces) tomato purée (optional)

2 large bay leaves

1 tablespoon imported Hungarian paprika

Roll meat in flour combined with salt and pepper. In a heavy pot or large skillet brown meat in oil over high heat, a few pieces at a time. Lower heat and sauté onions until transparent. Return meat to pan and add parsley, broth or soup, tomato purée, bay leaves, and paprika. Cover tightly and simmer slowly until meat is tender, about 2 hours. Stir once in a while, adding water if the sauce seems too thick.

Serves 4 to 6

Beef Bones Diable

SISI CAHAN
Development and Promotion

One need not throw out sparerib bones—they are very good if broiled until crisp and served with a piquant sauce.

6 leftover sparerib bones
Melted butter
Vinegar
Fine dry bread crumbs
½ cup prepared mustard
2 teaspoons dry mustard
3 tablespoons molasses
2 tablespoons vinegar
¼ cup Worcestershire sauce
½ teaspoon Tabasco
½ teaspoon salt

Dip the bones in melted butter mixed with vinegar. Roll in bread crumbs. Combine remaining ingredients for the sauce. Broil bones for 5 minutes, then begin basting with sauce and turning, continuing to broil and baste for 15 to 20 minutes, or until well browned.

Lamb Roast

PAMELA PATTERSON
Sales

A variation on chicken tandoori—the crust becomes black and seals in the juices.

1 leg of lamb, 5–6 pounds, trimmed of *all* fat and
   fell
1 teaspoon ground ginger
1 teaspoon garlic powder
1 teaspoon salt
1 teaspoon pepper
1 tablespoon tandoori mix or Dijon mustard
1 cup (½ pint) plain yogurt

Preheat oven to 375°.

Rub lamb with ginger, garlic powder, salt, pepper, and tandoori mix or mustard. Then completely coat with yogurt. Bake for 1½ hours for pink lamb. Coating will be crusty and black.

Serves 6

Boneless Lamb Wellington

FRAN KAPLAN
Sales

A shortcut, less expensive version of the classic beef Wellington, this is nevertheless fancy and good.

1 lamb shoulder, 3 pounds, boned and rolled, or
    1 leg of lamb, 4 pounds, boned and rolled
Salt and pepper
1 can (4 ounces) liver pâté
1½ tablespoons brandy
2 tablespoons sliced black pitted olives (optional)
2 cups biscuit mix
1 egg, beaten with 1 tablespoon water

Preheat oven to 350°.

Season lamb with salt and pepper and roast for 1½ to 2¼ hours (depending on whether you like it pink or well done). Cool to room temperature, remove string, and trim all excess fat. Stir the juices in the pan, season well, and set aside.

Combine the liver pâté with brandy and beat until fluffy. Spread over cooled lamb, and press in olives. Prepare biscuit mix according to directions on box. Roll out in rectangle as thinly as possible and invert lamb on center of dough, bringing up sides and ends. Make sure to encase completely. Trim off excess dough, moisten casing edges lightly with cold water, and press down to seal. Roll extra dough and shape into leaves or strips to decorate top of pastry. Brush with egg and water mixture. Bake at 425° for 15 minutes, or until pastry is golden brown. Reheat sauce and serve with meat.

Serves 6 to 8

Lamb Marrakech

INGE HECKEL
Development and Promotion

Originally from that bastion of Near Eastern elegance, the Mamounia Hotel in Marrakech. Serve with wheat pilaf.

4 pounds lean lamb, cut in 1½-inch cubes
   (preferably leg, but shoulder may be used)
½ cup olive oil
2 large onions, finely chopped
3 cloves garlic, minced in a garlic press
1 teaspoon cayenne pepper
2 teaspoons turmeric
2 cans (35 ounces each) whole peeled tomatoes
1 cup white raisins, soaked in sherry to cover
   until soft

In a large, heavy pot brown the lamb in the oil a few pieces at a time. Add the onion and garlic to brown lightly. Return lamb to pot. Add seasonings, tomatoes (with juice), raisins (with sherry), and bring to a boil. Cover and simmer for 1½ hours or until lamb is tender.

Serves 8

Lamb Shanks and String Beans

ANNETTE B. NEEDLE
Sculpture Reproduction Workshop

An Armenian recipe. Serve with Syrian bread, a hearty burgundy, and good friends.

4 lamb shanks
1 bunch leeks, sliced, or 2 medium onions, chopped
3 cloves garlic
4 medium, very ripe tomatoes, peeled and seeded,
   or one 16-ounce can whole tomatoes
1 bay leaf
1½ teaspoons ground cinnamon
Salt and freshly ground pepper
1 pound fresh, whole string beans
Chopped fresh parsley

50

soffietto

Trim excess fat from lamb shanks and melt it in a heavy skillet or Dutch oven. In it brown the shanks on all sides over high heat. Reduce heat, add leeks or onions and garlic, and cook until wilted but not browned. Add the tomatoes, bay leaf, cinnamon, salt and pepper to taste, and boiling water to barely cover. Simmer over very low heat, partially covered, for 1½ hours. Cool and refrigerate overnight. Skim off solidified fat, bring to a boil, add string beans, cover, and cook over medium heat until beans are tender. Sprinkle with freshly chopped parsley.

Serves 4

Lamb Pilaf
(with respects to the *New York Times*)

JOHANNA HECHT
Western European Arts

There are endless recipes for pilaf. This particular combination of spices makes it especially good.

¼ cup olive oil

1 pound boneless leg of lamb, cut into 1-inch cubes (shoulder may also be used, but be sure to cut away all the fat)

2 onions, finely chopped

2 cloves garlic, finely chopped

1 cup raw rice

⅓ cup currants

¼ cup pine nuts

3 cups chicken broth

⅛ teaspoon saffron (optional)

1 bay leaf, crumbled

½ stick cinnamon

⅛ teaspoon crushed coriander seed

⅛ teaspoon powdered cumin

Salt and freshly ground pepper

3 tablespoons chopped parsley

setaccio

51

Heat 2 tablespoons of the oil in a heavy casserole or Dutch oven and brown the lamb, a few pieces at a time. Set aside and keep warm. Add the remaining oil and the onions and garlic and cook until transparent. Add the rice and cook until it is golden and translucent, stirring constantly. Add the remaining ingredients except the parsley and bring to a boil. Return the lamb to the casserole, add the parsley, cover, and simmer until the liquid is absorbed and the rice done. Place the casserole in a warm place with a clean towel under the cover for 10 minutes. Remove the cinnamon stick. Serve.

Serves 4

barnchino

Kidneys in a Mustard Sauce

JACOB BEAN
Drawings

This marvelous dish must be done just before serving, but cooking it takes only 5 minutes. Serve it with steamed new potatoes.

16 lamb kidneys, split, white tubes and fat
   removed, and cut into small pieces
4 tablespoons butter
1 jigger brandy or whiskey
2 tablespoons Dijon mustard
½ pint heavy cream
Salt and freshly ground pepper

Sauté the kidneys in butter very quickly to desired degree of doneness, 1 or 2 minutes. Pour the brandy or whiskey over them and set afire, stirring vigorously until the flames die down. Immediately remove the kidneys from the pan with a slotted spoon to a warm dish. Add the mustard to the juices in the pan and stir over a low heat until a paste is formed. Slowly add the cream, stirring until smooth. Return the kidneys to the sauce and correct seasoning.

Serves 4

Veal Casserole with Peas

EDWARD M. M. WARBURG
Vice-Director for Public Affairs

This and Curried Eggs (page 118) are amongst my wife's favorite recipes. Serve the casserole with toasted French bread and red or white wine. A simple dessert should follow.

5 pounds veal, cut in 1½-inch cubes
2 tablespoons butter
16 small new potatoes, peeled and thinly sliced
3 pounds white onions, peeled and thinly sliced
1 bunch carrots, peeled and thinly sliced
Salt and freshly ground pepper
Chicken stock, fresh or canned (if necessary)
1 pint sour cream
1 can French peas, drained
Chopped parsley

Preheat oven to 350°.

In a skillet brown the veal lightly in the butter. In a large buttered casserole dish place layers of the following, in this order: veal, potatoes, onions, carrots. Sprinkle each layer of carrots with a little salt and pepper. Repeat layers until casserole is almost full. Cook, uncovered, in oven for 2 hours. Baste from time to time by inserting a bulb baster at the side of the casserole and squeezing the juice on top. Be sure not to disturb the layers. If the casserole appears to get dry, add a little chicken stock. Remove casserole from oven and spread sour cream thickly on top. Then pour the peas in the center of the sour cream, pyramid fashion. Do not put the casserole in the oven again; its heat will warm the sour cream and peas. Sprinkle with chopped parsley.

Serves 8

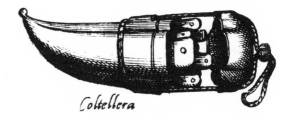

Coltellera

53

Casserole of Veal

DRACIA FEATHERMAN
Junior Museum

Serve with buttered noodles and tossed salad.

2 ½ – 3 pounds veal cutlet, cut into cubes
3 tablespoons butter
1 tablespoon oil
2 tablespoons chopped onion
1 clove garlic, chopped
2 tablespoons flour
1 cup chicken stock
1 cup dry white wine (more if necessary)
4 large tomatoes, peeled (or one 16-ounce can
   tomatoes, drained)
Juice of 1 lemon
Salt and pepper to taste
1 pound mushrooms, sliced

Preheat oven to 350°.

Brown the veal cubes in 3 tablespoons of butter and the oil in a heavy skillet. Remove meat with a slotted spoon and place in a casserole. In the same fat sauté the onion and garlic until transparent. Stir in the flour until smooth and add the chicken broth, ¼ cup of the wine, tomatoes, lemon juice, and salt and pepper to taste. Pour this mixture over the veal. Cover the casserole and simmer for 1 ½ hours, adding the balance of the wine as seems necessary. Sauté the mushrooms quickly in butter and spread them over the meat. Return the casserole to the oven for an additional 30 to 45 minutes.

Best if made the day before and refrigerated overnight. In this case, bring the casserole to room temperature and add the sautéed mushrooms just before reheating.

Serves 6

Veal in Cream

MARGOT FEELY
Publications

From Joan Apter, a former assistant in this department. Serve with rice.

Veal scallops for 4
Flour
Salt
3 tablespoons butter
2 cups sliced mushrooms
Juice of 1 lemon
½ teaspoon sugar
1 tablespoon dried tarragon
1 cup heavy cream
Freshly ground pepper
Finely chopped parsley

Dip the veal scallops in flour seasoned with a pinch of salt. Brown the scallops in 2 tablespoons butter over a very hot flame, about 2 minutes to a side. Remove them from pan. Add the remaining butter and sauté the mushrooms with a little salt, stirring until they are limp, about 2 minutes. Remove from pan. In the same pan add lemon juice and sugar, and stir with a wire whisk until mixture sizzles. Add tarragon and cream and continue to stir until mixture is smooth. Make sure to scrape any coagulated juices from the side of the pan into the sauce. Return the veal and mushrooms to the pan (with any juice they may have made), add pepper, and correct seasoning. Simmer for 15 minutes, stirring often with a wooden spoon. Sprinkle with parsley.

Can be covered and kept warm for about 30 minutes.

Serves 4

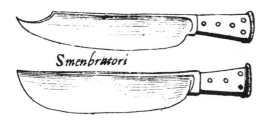

Smenbratori

Mock Baby Bear Fillets

KNUD NIELSEN
Conservation

A Swiss recipe.

3 thin pork tenderloins
Red wine
2 cloves garlic, crushed
1 teaspoon sea salt
1 tablespoon freshly picked pine needles, rinsed
Dash sugar
Butter

Place the meat, wine to cover it, garlic, salt, pine needles, and sugar in a nonmetallic bowl and marinate for one week in the refrigerator. Slice the meat into thin slivers and sauté in butter until brown.

Serves 5 to 6

Sweet and Sour Pork

BARBARA A. DOUGHERTY
Personnel

Exotic if served with fried rice.

½ cup flour
1½ tablespoons ginger
3½ pounds pork shoulder, trimmed of excess fat
   and cut into small cubes
¾ cup sesame oil
2 cans (13½ ounces each) pineapple chunks
½ cup flour
½ cup white vinegar
½ cup soy sauce
1 tablespoon Worcestershire sauce
Sugar
1 tablespoon salt
1 teaspoon pepper
¾ cup thinly sliced carrots

pignatta a bussola

2 medium green peppers, seeded and cut into
strips
1 can (1 pound) bean sprouts, drained (or an
equivalent amount of fresh)
1 can (8½ ounces) water chestnuts, drained and
thinly sliced
1 tablespoon chili powder

Mix the flour and ginger and coat pork thoroughly with mixture. Heat oil in a large skillet and brown meat on all sides, a few pieces at a time. Drain the juice from the pineapple chunks, supplement juice with water to measure 1¾ cups liquid in all, and gradually add to flour, stirring until smooth. Pour into skillet in which meat was browned, and add vinegar, soy sauce, and Worcestershire. Heat to boiling, stirring constantly, and boil 1 minute. Stir in sugar to taste, salt and pepper, and add meat. Reduce heat, cover, and simmer for 45 minutes, or until meat is tender. Stir occasionally. Add the pineapple chunks, carrots, green pepper, and bean sprouts and cook uncovered for 30 minutes. Add the water chestnuts and chili powder, stir, and serve.

Serves 6 to 8

Marinade for Pork

HUGH R. CLOPTON
Superintendent's Office

Marinate pork that you intend to roast or bake for 2 hours.

½ cup honey
½ cup soy sauce
1 teaspoon powdered ginger
½ teaspoon dry mustard
1 tablespoon brown sugar

Combine all ingredients.

Herbed Meat Loaf

KNUD NIELSEN
Conservation

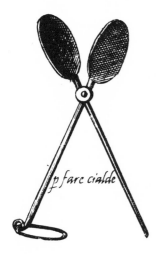

Collecting the many ingredients is quite a job, but well worth it.

1½ cups milk

Liquid from a 4-ounce can of mushrooms

2 eggs, beaten

2 tablespoons Moselle wine mustard

2 tablespoons powdered mushrooms

2 tablespoons bottled horseradish, drained

¼ teaspoon garlic powder

3–4 dashes cayenne pepper

1½ tablespoons sea salt or regular salt

2 teaspoons paprika

1 teaspoon sage poultry seasoning

8 slices sesame diet bread, chopped, rinsed quickly
   in water, and squeezed

4 pounds ground chuck

1½ pounds ground lean pork

3 medium onions, finely chopped

1 teaspoon dried mint, freshly pestled

1 teaspoon dried rosemary, freshly pestled

2 tablespoons dried basil

Several fresh or canned mushroom caps

1 pint heavy cream, half-and-half, or milk

Preheat oven to 350°.

Place the first 11 ingredients in a bowl, stir well, and let stand. In another bowl combine the moistened bread with the ground meat and add onions. Combine the two mixtures, divide, and place into loaf pans, making sure that there are no air bubbles. Sprinkle the loaves with herbs and insert a ridge of mushroom caps down the center of each. Bake for 1¼ to 1½ hours. Remove loaves from pans and over low flame rinse each one with ½ pint cream or milk, stirring in all the brown residue. Season to taste and serve sauce with meat loaf.

The meat loaf is best if the combined ingredients are refrigerated overnight before cooking. Can be frozen.

Serves 4 to 6 (each loaf)

Bloody Mary Meat Loaf

SHEILAH CROSS
High School Programs

Bloody Mary mix is an unlikely ingredient for meat loaf, but the result is spicy and moist. Very good hot and also excellent cold (like a country pâté) for a picnic, served with cornichons.

> 5 pounds ground meat: about one-third each of
>   veal, pork, and beef
> 1 cup bread crumbs
> 3 eggs
> ½ cup ketchup
> 1½ cups liquid Bloody Mary mix
> 4 bay leaves, roughly crumbled
> 2 tablespoons thyme, crumbled
> ½ cup chopped parsley
> 2 onions, minced (optional)
> Salt and freshly ground pepper
> Uncooked bacon strips

Preheat oven to 325°.

Mix all ingredients except bacon and form into two loaves (one can be frozen and served later). Place in terrines (makes a nice shape) or loaf pans. Lay bacon on top to cover and bake for 1¼ hours. Drain any accumulated fat. If serving cold, remove bacon and invert loaf; some jelly glaze will appear on top.

Serves 8 (each loaf)

Sausage and Potato Casserole

MARIAN HARRISON
Catalogue

This recipe derives from a traditional Hungarian peasant dish, *rakott krumpli*. It is usually served for lunch with a hearty salad of cabbage, cucumbers, spices, paprika, salt, and vinegar.

59

stufatoro

4 potatoes, peeled and thinly sliced

8 Italian sweet sausage links (2 packages), cut in
   1-inch slices

1 medium onion, peeled and thinly sliced

1 pint sour cream

4 hard-boiled eggs, sliced or halved

Salt and freshly ground pepper

Preheat oven to 375°.

Butter a casserole dish and add layers of the following, in this order: potatoes, sausage meat, onion, sour cream (be generous), and eggs. Sprinkle egg layer very lightly with salt and pepper. Repeat layering process to top of casserole, ending with a layer of sour cream. Bake, uncovered, for 1 to 1¼ hours, or until potatoes are tender.

Any leftover casserole can be successfully reheated.

Serves 4

Bitki

BRADFORD KELLEHER
Publications

Of Russian origin—a glamorous way to use chopped beef.

4 slices white bread

½ cup milk

1 pound ground beef chuck

Salt and pepper to taste

¼ teaspoon nutmeg

2 medium onions, thinly sliced

2 tablespoons butter

½ pint sour cream

Soak slices of bread in milk until soggy. Squeeze out milk, crumble, and mix with meat. Add salt, pepper, and nutmeg, and mix thoroughly. Form into balls about 2½ inches in diameter. In a large, heavy skillet sauté the onions slowly in the butter. When transparent remove and place meatballs in pan. Brown on all sides, reduce heat to very low, spread onions over meatballs, and cover.

Cook for 20 to 25 minutes, turning once. Remove excess fat with bulb baster, and stir in the sour cream. Heat thoroughly but do not boil. Serve.

This dish can be made beforehand by cooking partially and finishing 5 to 10 minutes before serving.

Serves 4

Pastichio

CYNTHIA LAMBROS
Drawings

A Greek dish. Serve with a salad for a party.

2 onions, chopped
1 clove garlic, minced
4 tablespoons butter
3 pounds ground beef
1 teaspoon cinnamon
½ teaspoon nutmeg
1 can (8 ounces) tomato sauce
½ cup sherry or white wine
1 pound no. 1 spaghetti
4 tablespoons melted butter
3 eggs, beaten
2½ cups grated Romano cheese
Salt and pepper
1 cup chicken broth
4 cups béchamel sauce
Cinnamon

butiglia

mortaro

Preheat oven to 350°.

Sauté the onions and garlic in butter until transparent. Add the beef, crumbled, and brown it. Add the cinnamon, nutmeg, tomato sauce, and wine, and simmer for 30 minutes. In the meantime cook the spaghetti, drain, and mix with melted butter and beaten eggs. Spread half the spaghetti on the bottom of a greased baking pan (15½ by 10½ by 2¼ inches). Sprinkle with ¼ cup of the grated cheese, salt, and pepper. Cover the spaghetti with the meat mixture

61

and sprinkle with another ¼ cup grated cheese, salt, and pepper. Mix the chicken broth and the remaining 2 cups of grated cheese into the béchamel sauce and spread over the final layer of spaghetti. Sprinkle very lightly with cinnamon and bake for 1 hour, or until top is golden brown. Cut into squares.

Can be assembled early in the day and cooked before serving.

Serves 10 to 12

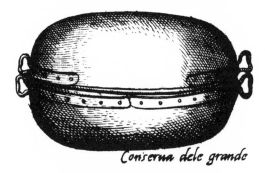

Conserua dele grande

Chicken Scaloppine

PAMELA PATTERSON
Sales

An economical and delicious alternative to veal.

  2 whole chicken breasts
  2 eggs, well beaten
  Bread crumbs (fresh or dried)
  ¼ pound butter
  Minced parsley
  Lemon wedges

Split and bone the chicken breasts, slice each piece in half horizontally, making 8 pieces in all, and flatten (a butcher can do this). Combine the eggs with ¼ cup water, and dip the breasts in the mixture. Coat them with bread crumbs and lay on a cookie sheet to dry for 10 minutes. Heat the butter to bubbling in a black cast-iron skillet, and quickly sauté chicken until golden brown. Drain, sprinkle with parsley, and serve immediately with lemon wedges.

Serves 4

Chicken and Dumplings

ANITA MULLER
Sales

Adapted from a German recipe. The chicken and sauce can be prepared well in advance; the dumplings should be cooked just before serving.

CHICKEN
1 chicken or capon (about 6 pounds)
3 stalks celery
1 large onion, sliced
2 carrots, sliced
4 stalks parsley
2 bay leaves
Salt and pepper

SAUCE
3 cups chicken broth
6 tablespoons butter
6 tablespoons flour
1½ teaspoons salt
½ teaspoon pepper

DUMPLINGS
1½ cups flour
¾ teaspoon salt
2¼ teaspoons baking powder
2 teaspoons butter or margarine
¾ cup milk

Chicken. Clean chicken and put into a large kettle or stewing pot with celery, onion, carrots, parsley, bay leaves, and sprinklings of salt and pepper. Add cold water barely to cover, bring to a boil, and simmer, partially covered, for 1 to 1½ hours, until meat is ready to fall off the bones. Remove chicken from broth, take off skin, and separate meat from bones in large pieces; set aside. Return the bones to the broth and continue to simmer for another 30 minutes. Correct seasoning, cool broth, strain it, and skim off fat (if chicken is cooked well in advance, place cooled broth in the refrigerator and skim off solidified fat several hours later).

Sauce. Heat 3 cups of chicken broth. Melt butter in large pan and add flour. Blend into a smooth roux, being careful that it does not color. Gradually add the heated broth, stirring constantly. When

63

smooth, lower heat and simmer as slowly as possible for 20 minutes, occasionally skimming off the film that forms on the surface. Season carefully with salt and pepper. Add chicken pieces to hot sauce. If dish is to be served immediately, bring to a gentle boil; if made in advance, cool and refrigerate.

Dumplings. Sift the flour with the salt and baking powder. Work in the butter or margarine with a fork until the mixture is crumbly. Add the milk, and work into a dough with a fork. When the chicken and sauce are bubbling gently, form dumplings with a tablespoon and drop them into the sauce. Cover and cook over low to moderate heat for 15 minutes (if the sauce boils too fast, the dumplings will be doughy). Serve.

Serves 4

Baked Chicken with Apple Stuffing

ROBIE ROGGE
Publications

A recipe for the fall—the apples should be fresh and tart.

½ pound butter

1 large onion, finely chopped

¼ cup chopped celery

4 McIntosh apples, peeled, cored, and diced

1 cup coarsely chopped almonds

½ cup raisins

1 cup soft bread crumbs

1 teaspoon salt

½ teaspoon pepper

1 teaspoon grated lemon rind

½ teaspoon coriander

½ teaspoon thyme

¼ teaspoon marjoram

½ teaspoon nutmeg

3 whole chicken breasts, split

Flour

Salt and pepper

Preheat oven to 350°.

Melt half the butter (¼ pound) in a skillet, and sauté onion until transparent. Add celery, apples, and almonds. Cover raisins with boiling water and let stand a minute; drain and add to onion mixture. Stir in bread crumbs, salt, pepper, lemon rind, coriander, thyme, marjoram, and nutmeg, and mix well. Spread in the bottom of a pan (9 by 13 by 2 inches). Melt the remaining butter in the same skillet. Shake the chicken in a bag with flour, salt, and pepper. Brown chicken breasts, place on top of apple stuffing, cover with foil, and bake 10 minutes. Remove foil and bake an additional 15 minutes.

The stuffing can be made well in advance; the chicken should be cooked just before serving.

Serves 6

Chicken Napoleone

FRANK ANDRIANO
Security

The cognac or whiskey gives this simple dish a rich flavor that distinguishes the recipe from many others like it.

> 1 frying chicken, cut into pieces
> ½ cup olive oil
> 2 tablespoons cognac or whiskey
> ½ cup white wine
> 1 clove garlic, peeled
> 2–3 tomatoes (or an equivalent amount of
>   canned), peeled and chopped
> Salt and pepper
> Chopped parsley

Wash the chicken pieces and dry with paper towels. Heat the oil to very hot in a frying pan, and brown the chicken in it for about 5 minutes, turning pieces a couple of times. Pour off most of the oil and add the cognac or whiskey, stirring. Add the wine, garlic, tomatoes, and salt and pepper to taste. Cover and simmer for about 30 minutes. Remove garlic clove, pour into a serving dish, and sprinkle with parsley.

Serves 4

Chicken with Red Pepper Sauce

ANITA MULLER
Sales

The peppers must be sweet red ones—green peppers will not give the same flavor.

SAUCE
- 1 clove garlic, minced
- Olive oil
- 4 sweet red peppers, seeded and cut into ½-inch pieces
- 4 medium ripe tomatoes, seeded and cut into ½-inch pieces
- ½ teaspoon basil
- ½ teaspoon oregano
- Salt and pepper
- 1½ six-ounce cans tomato paste

CHICKEN
- 6 whole chicken breasts, split
- 3 tablespoons butter
- Salt and pepper

Sauce. Sauté the garlic in enough oil to cover bottom of pan. When oil begins to smoke and garlic is slightly browned, add the red peppers and sauté until they begin to wilt, but don't overcook. Add the tomatoes and herbs and continue to cook until the vegetables are tender but firm. Season to taste. Stir in the tomato paste and mix well.

Chicken. Sauté the chicken breasts in the butter until brown. Season with salt and pepper and cook about 20 minutes or until done. Remove to heated platter and pour hot sauce over them. Serve.

The sauce can be done well in advance; the chicken should be cooked and the dish assembled just before serving.

Serves 6 amply

Stuffed Chicken Breast

PATRICIA GORSLINE
Payroll

Invented while trying to find something new to do with chicken. Serve with sautéed mushrooms and rice.

> 1 slice Swiss cheese, halved
> 1 slice ham, halved
> 1 whole chicken breast, split, boned, and flattened
> 1 egg beaten with 1 tablespoon water
> Bread crumbs
> Salt and pepper
> 3 tablespoons butter

Preheat oven to 350°.

Place a slice of cheese and ham on each chicken cutlet. Roll the three layers up and secure with a toothpick. Combine the egg and water mixture. Dip rolls into the egg and then the bread crumbs. Brown in the butter and bake until golden brown, about 20 minutes.

Serves 2

Poddyng of Capou(n) Necke

JOHN MCKENDRY
Prints and Photographs

From Maxime McKendry's collection of English recipes, many of which appear in her *Seven Centuries Cookbook* (McGraw Hill, 1973). Adapted from *Two Fifteenth Century Cookery Books*, edited by Thomas Austin. The original manuscript is in the British Museum, London, and dates from 1430–1440. About this recipe Mrs. McKendry writes, "My New York butcher was not the least surprised when I told him about the medieval sausages I was about to make with his chicken necks. 'Oh,' he said, 'my mother was German and used to make that dish for us often . . . I can't get my wife to make it!' So I discovered that this delicious, economical dish was still around, seven centuries later."

   "Take Percely, gysour, & the leuer of the herte, & perboyle in fayre water; than choppe hem smal, & put raw yolkys of Eyroun .ij. or .iij. ther-to, & choppe for-with. Take Maces and Clowes, &

put ther-to, & Safroun, & a lytil Pepir, & Salt; & fille hym vppe & sew hym, & lay him a-long on the capon Bakke, & prycke him ther-on, and roste hym, & serue f[orth]."

Skin of a chicken or capon neck, removed from
   the bone
1 chicken gizzard, boiled
1 chicken heart, boiled
1 raw chicken liver
1 hard-boiled egg yolk, chopped
1 pinch saffron
1 pinch mace
1 pinch cloves
Salt and pepper to taste
1 tablespoon chopped parsley

Skewer or sew one end of the neck skin. Chop the gizzard, heart, and liver finely, and mix thoroughly with the rest of the ingredients. Fill the skin with the mixture and secure the other end, forming a fat sausage. Bake in the same pan with the bird or skewer sausage onto its back. Baste it when you baste the bird.

The neck bone, boiled in the water that cooked the gizzard and heart, will produce a tasty broth for your gravy.

Valencian Paella

CARMEN GOMEZ-MORENO
Medieval Art

If a seafood paella is preferred, replace the chicken with eel, very tasty but unfortunately disliked by most Americans. Scallops and squids are also successful. Spanish rice does not cook well in America. If you are lucky with Carolina rice, use it; otherwise Uncle Ben is always reliable. Remember that rice in paella should never be overcooked. The paella can be kept warm in a low oven until ready to serve. Que Aproveche!

1 frying chicken, cut up

1 carrot, peeled

1 onion, peeled

1 pound mussels, scrubbed and debearded, or clams

2 medium onions, chopped

10 tablespoons oil

1 green pepper, chopped

1 can habas or fava beans or peas

5 ounces fresh pork or ham, diced

6 Italian sweet sausages (*not* chorizo or peperoni),
   cut into 1-inch pieces

2 cups raw rice

5 cups broth (from chicken and mussels, supple-
   mented by chicken stock, if necessary)

Salt

Pinch saffron

1 tablespoon chopped parsley

1–2 cloves garlic (to taste), minced

Few drops lemon juice

½ pound shrimp, cleaned

1 green pepper, roasted (or preserved and seasoned
   red peppers)

Several hearts of artichokes

le carda

Place the chicken, carrot, and onion in a large pot, cover with water, and simmer for about 20 minutes. Remove, and reserve the broth. In a frying pan cover the mussels with water, bring to a boil, and cook until they open. Remove them, and reserve the broth.

In another frying pan sauté the onion in 5 tablespoons of the oil until it starts to turn golden. Add the chopped pepper, habas or fava beans, and pork or ham. Cover and simmer very slowly for 6 or 7 minutes. Add the chicken and sausage, cover, and cook for another 3 minutes.

Heat remaining 5 tablespoons of oil in a paella pan (a flat, low pan, usually made of iron, with two handles). Add the rice and move the pan continuously until it sounds like sand; be careful not to let it turn golden. Heat 5 cups of broth to boiling with salt to taste, saffron, parsley, and garlic, and add it to the rice along with the sautéed mixture. Bring rapidly to a boil and cook for 5 minutes. Add

stufatoro

the lemon juice. Without disturbing the rice, place the mussels and shrimp on top, distributed as artistically as possible. Continue to cook, and complete the decoration with the pepper and artichokes. Keep moving the pan frequently. When the liquid starts to diminish, lower the flame. After a total cooking time of 15 minutes turn the heat off, cover the pan, and let it rest for 5 minutes. Uncover and let it rest 6 minutes before serving.

Serves 8

Rock Cornish Game Hen
Stuffed with Wild Rice

ANITA MULLER
Sales

For a dinner party. The stuffing can be considered as a vegetable, so you need only a salad.

STUFFING	12 ounces (2 packages) long-grain wild rice
	2 medium onions, sliced
	½ cup chopped celery
	½ cup chopped green peppers
	1 cup chopped mushrooms
	¼ pound butter
	½ cup sliced water chestnuts
	½ cup raisins soaked in brandy
BIRDS	6 rock Cornish game hens (about 1 pound each), preferably fresh
	Salt and pepper
	Butter
	1 jar apricot preserves
	1 tablespoon brandy
	½ cup chicken stock

Preheat oven to 400°.

Stuffing. Cook rice according to directions on package. Sauté the onions, celery, peppers, and mushrooms in butter until soft and add water chestnuts and raisins. Mix with rice.

70

Birds. Rub hens inside and out with salt and pepper. Stuff them with the rice mixture. Rub with butter and roast for 25 minutes, basting every so often until they are lightly browned. Lower heat to 350° and roast for 25 minutes longer, continuing to baste. In the meantime, melt the preserves in a small pan and add the brandy. Using a pastry brush, glaze the birds with the mixture and cook for 10 minutes more. The juices should run clear. Remove birds to a serving dish and keep warm. Pour the stock into the roasting pan, and over a high heat stir vigorously, scraping the coagulated juices into the sauce. When it is sufficiently reduced and has a strong flavor, season it well and serve with the hens.

Serves 6

Bourbon-Flavored Pheasant
(with respects to Elizabeth David)

JAMES PARKER
Western European Arts

1 pheasant, trussed
Salt
2 tablespoons butter
Freshly ground pepper
2 ounces bourbon whiskey
½ pint heavy cream
Chopped parsley

Preheat oven to 350°.

Rub the pheasant with salt. Melt the butter in a heavy metal pan, and roast the pheasant in it for about 45 minutes, basting often and turning it several times so that all sides are well browned. Carve the bird, season the pieces with salt and pepper, and arrange on a warm serving platter. Place in a warm oven.

Warm the bourbon. Heat up the juices in the pan, add the bourbon, and set a match to it, tilting it until the flames have burned out. Add the cream and stir over the heat until the sauce thickens. Check seasoning. Pour sauce over the pheasant, and sprinkle with a good handful of parsley.

Serves 2 to 3

nauicella cō piaſt relle et 4 piédi

Pheasant Hash

DANIEL P. DAVISON
Trustee

Katushe and Danny Davison have lived in London for the past several years and have found themselves in the enviable predicament of having their freezer bulging with pheasants. They invented this excellent dish, which can be served at the most intimate as well as at the grandest dinner. For those of us who aren't apt to have a surplus of pheasants, chicken or even leftover turkey adapts very well.

2 pheasants, cooked (approximately 4 cups of meat)
Butter
3 tablespoons flour
2 cups pheasant or chicken stock (or milk)
Salt and pepper
Approximately 1 cup dry white wine or champagne
6 bacon strips, fried until crisp, then crumbled
4 pieces whole wheat bread, crusts removed, and
    quartered

Preheat oven to 375°.

Cook pheasants in any way you wish. It is best to boil them gently with vegetables and water so that the stock may be used for the hash's sauce, but if you choose to roast them, canned chicken stock or milk can be used. Allow birds to cool, and remove meat. Chop coarsely and put half of it through the meat grinder, on coarse mince. In a large skillet melt 2 tablespoons of butter and stir in the flour to make a roux. Heat the stock or milk to just boiling, add to roux, and stir until thickened and smooth. Cook as slowly as possible for about 20 minutes, skimming off the film that forms on top. Season carefully. Combine the sauce with the chopped and ground pheasant, and add wine or champagne (be careful not to kill the taste of the meat). Pour into a white soufflé dish, spread the bacon bits over the hash, and heat for 30 minutes. In the meantime, sauté the bread quarters in butter and keep warm. When the hash is bubbly stand the toast spikes into it, wrap a damask napkin around the dish, and serve.

   The hash may be made well in advance and refrigerated (even frozen), but the bacon should be cooked, crumbled, and sprinkled on top just before heating and serving.

Serves 4

Goose à la Morton Muller
(Goose Stuffed with Turkey)

ANITA MULLER
Sales

The two kinds of poultry complement each other, a goose being fat and a turkey breast dry by nature. Both profit from being cooked together. Invented for a family in which the parents liked goose while the children preferred the white meat of turkey.

> 1 goose (12–15 pounds)
> Powdered ginger
> Lemon juice
> Salt and pepper
> 1 boneless breast of turkey, fresh or frozen and
>   thawed
> 2 knob celeries, quartered
> 2 medium onions, quartered
> 2 medium McIntosh apples, peeled, cored, and
>   quartered
> 2 carrots, peeled and sliced lengthwise

Preheat oven to 400°.

Roast the unstuffed goose on a rack in a roasting pan for 20 to 30 minutes. Prick the bird frequently to release as much fat as possible. Remove fat from the pan, and reduce oven heat to 325°.

Rub the outside and cavity of the goose with ginger, lemon juice, salt, and pepper. Place the turkey breast in the cavity and distribute the vegetables around the goose. Roast it 15 minutes per pound, until the skin is a rich brown.

Serves 6

tortera con il coperto

Rolled Fillet of Sole

PAMELA PATTERSON
Sales

Very light—a snappy first course or for a lunch.

1 onion, minced

2 tablespoons butter

1 cup fresh bread crumbs

¼ cup minced parsley

Salt and pepper

3 drops Tabasco sauce

1 tablespoon brown mustard

½ pound lump crab meat

½ cup heavy cream

4 fillets of sole, halved down center

Dry white wine

White grapes, halved (optional)

Preheat oven to 375°.

Sauté the onion in butter until translucent. Add bread crumbs, parsley, salt and pepper to taste, Tabasco, and mustard, and toss. Remove from heat and add crab meat; then add cream. Lay out half a fillet and spoon on stuffing. Roll and secure with a toothpick. Repeat with all fillets, and lay rolls on their sides in a very shallow baking dish; pour in wine just to cover bottom. Add a sprinkling of white grapes if you wish. Bake for 20 to 25 minutes, until fish flakes. If desired, run under broiler to brown tops lightly.

Can be assembled well in advance and cooked just before serving.

Serves 8 as an appetizer, **4** as a main course

piastrella

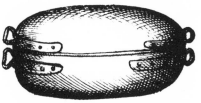

Conserua mezana

foratoro colmanico

Stuffed Striped Bass

ELIZABETH FLINN
Junior Museum

The pine nuts make this special.

> 4 slices fresh bread, crumbled
> 1 egg
> 1 small onion, chopped
> 2 tablespoons chopped fresh dill
> 1 teaspoon dried thyme
> ¼ cup pine nuts
> 4 tablespoons butter
> Salt and pepper
> 1 striped bass (about 4 pounds), cleaned (have fish
>   market leave head and tail on as decoration, if
>   you wish)
> Celery leaves
> 3 slices bacon

Preheat oven to 500°.

Combine the bread crumbs, egg, onion, dill, thyme, pine nuts, butter, and salt and pepper to taste, and stuff fish with mixture. Place fish on a bed of celery leaves and cover it with the slices of bacon. Bake for 10 minutes at 500°, lower heat to 400° and bake for 40 minutes, or 10 minutes per pound.

Serves 4

75

Baked Stuffed Salmon

JOHN MCKENDRY
Prints and Photographs

From Maxime McKendry's collection of English recipes, many of which appear in her *Seven Centuries Cookbook* (McGraw Hill, 1973). Adapted from *The Accomplisht Cook, or the Art and Mystery of Cooking* by Robert May, printed in London for Obadiah Blagrave at the Bear and Star in St. Paul's Church-Yard, 1685. A prerequisite for this recipe is an herb garden!

¼ cup chopped onion
½ cup chopped fresh thyme
¼ cup chopped fresh rosemary
½ cup chopped fresh savory
½ cup chopped fresh marjoram
1 clove garlic, minced
1 teaspoon nutmeg
1 salmon or striped bass (3–4 pounds), cleaned and boned
1 cup dry white wine
1 bay leaf, crumbled
Salt and pepper
2 anchovies, crushed
6 tablespoons butter

Preheat oven to 375°.

Thoroughly blend together the onion, herbs, garlic, and nutmeg, and stuff the salmon with the mixture. Pour the wine into the bottom of a baking dish, adding the bay leaf, salt and pepper to taste, and anchovies. You will need very little extra salt because of the anchovies. Melt 4 tablespoons of the butter for basting. Place the fish in the dish and bake for 30 to 35 minutes, or until the fish flakes easily, basting with the melted butter. Put the fish on a warmed serving dish and remove skin. Keep warm while reducing the liquid in which it was cooked by half over a sharp flame. Strain, beat in the remaining 2 tablespoons of butter over a low flame, and pour this sauce over the fish.

Serves 4 to 6

Halibut Baked with Lemon

CLARE VINCENT
Western European Arts

For those who have to produce something interesting after a long day's work.

> 3–4 lemons, sliced
> 4 slices halibut, fresh or frozen and thawed
> Salt and pepper
> 2 cups (1 pint) sour cream
> Chopped parsley

Preheat oven to 375°.

Line a glass baking dish or pie plate with lemon slices. Lay fish on top of them and bake for about 40 minutes, or until fish is flaky at the edges. Sprinkle with salt and pepper to taste. Then cover the fish with sour cream and bake for another 10 to 15 minutes. Remove from the lemon slices, sprinkle with parsley, and serve immediately.

Serves 4

Fish Cooked in Foil

THEODORE ROUSSEAU
Vice-Director, Curator in Chief

The credit really goes to my assistant, Rosemary Levai.

> Salt and pepper
> Butter or oil
> 1 fish fillet or steak per person
> Any of the following: chopped shallots, scallions,
>   fresh parsley, dill, thin slices of green pepper,
>   tarragon, basil, anything

Preheat oven to 350°.

Tear pieces of foil large enough to enclose each fish fillet. Sprinkle each piece of foil with salt, pepper, and a very small dab of butter or oil. Place fish in the middle of the foil. Sprinkle herbs, etc., on top of the fish, and add another dab of butter, salt, and pepper. Wrap foil to enclose fish in a leakproof package, place on a cookie sheet, and bake for 20 to 30 minutes. Unwrap carefully, allowing juices to run out onto the serving plate.

Crabs Butter'd

JOHN MCKENDRY
Prints and Photographs

From Maxime McKendry's collection of English recipes, many of which appear in her *Seven Centuries Cookbook* (McGraw Hill, 1973). Adapted from *The London Art of Cookery* by John Farley, principal cook at the London Tavern, printed in London for Scratcher and Letterman, Ave-Maria Lane, 1804.

> 2 tablespoons butter
> 1 pound crab meat
> ½ cup white wine
> 1 tablespoon sherry
> ½ teaspoon pepper
> 1 teaspoon salt
> ½ teaspoon grated nutmeg
> ½ teaspoon ginger
> ¼ cup bread crumbs
> 2 tablespoons lemon juice
> Lemon slices

Melt the butter and cook the crab meat in it gently, without browning. Add the wine, sherry, pepper, salt, nutmeg, ginger, and bread crumbs, mix well, and simmer for a few minutes until the crab meat is done. Add the lemon juice and cook a few seconds longer. Fill ramekins or scallop shells with this mixture, and garnish with lemon slices.

If not to be served at once, dot with a few small pieces of butter and reheat in a 375° oven.

Serves 3 to 4

Lobster Thermidor

ERIC ZAFRAN
European Paintings

My mother's best recipe.

Butter
½ cup sherry
2 cups cooked lobster meat
3–4 tablespoons flour
1½ cups milk
4 egg yolks, well beaten
1 cup sliced mushrooms
Pimento (optional)
½ teaspoon salt
½ cup bread crumbs
2 tablespoons freshly grated Parmesan cheese

Preheat oven to 300°.

Melt ¼ cup of butter and add the sherry; boil 1 minute. Add the lobster and set aside. In the top of a double boiler over simmering water melt ⅓ cup of butter. Stir in the flour until smooth. Drain the liquid from the lobster, and slowly add it to the roux along with the milk. When smooth, cook for several minutes. Stir ½ cup of the hot sauce into the egg yolks, then return the mixture to the double boiler, beating well; do not allow to boil. Cook 3 to 4 minutes. Add the lobster, mushrooms, pimento if wished, and salt. Pour into a large casserole dish. Melt ¼ cup of butter. Combine with bread crumbs and cheese, sprinkle over top. Bake 15 to 20 minutes, until well heated.

Serves 4

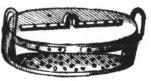

Chinese Shrimp and Vegetables

FONG CHOW
Far Eastern Art

Mr. Chow and his wife chose this dish from their collection of Chinese recipes because, while the flavor is absolutely authentic, the ingredients are simple and available anywhere.

1 tablespoon cornstarch

4 tablespoons peanut or corn oil

1 onion, cut into ¾-inch pieces

1 pound fresh raw shrimp, shelled and deveined

1 green pepper, cut into ¾-inch pieces

2 stalks celery, cut into ¾-inch pieces

1 carrot, cut on the bias into pieces ¾ inch long, ⅛ inch thick

6 tablespoons ketchup

1 tablespoon soy sauce

1 tablespoon sherry

1 tablespoon chili powder (optional—for a spicier dish)

Dissolve the cornstarch in 3 tablespoons of water and set aside. Heat the oil in a frying pan over a high flame. Add the onion and stir for about 1 minute. Add the shrimp and continue stirring until they turn pink, 1 to 2 minutes. Add the vegetables and stir a few times. Add the remaining ingredients, mix, and bring to a boil. Cover and cook over a medium flame for 2 minutes. Add the cornstarch mixture and stir slowly until the sauce thickens. Continue cooking for 1 minute after the boiling point is reached. Serve.

Serves 4

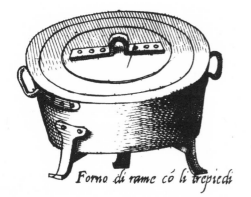

Forno di rame có li trepiedi

Coquilles St. Jacques Parmentier

DAVID SCHIFF
Trustee

A fringe of mashed potatoes makes a variation on this elegant dish.

1½ pounds bay scallops
1½ cups white wine
½ bay leaf
1 teaspoon salt
½ pound butter
4 tablespoons flour
½ teaspoon white pepper
½ teaspoon nutmeg
4 potatoes, peeled and quartered
Red pepper or paprika

Bring the scallops, white wine, bay leaf, and salt to a simmer, and cook gently for about 5 minutes, until the scallops are done (be very careful not to overcook them!). Remove the scallops to a dish with a slotted spoon, reserving the broth. In another pan melt ¼ pound of the butter and mix in the flour to form a roux. Cook, without browning, for a minute or so. Add the broth, stirring, until you have a smooth sauce. Add the scallops, and season with pepper and nutmeg. Divide mixture into 4 coquille shells or ramekins.

Boil the potatoes, drain, and mash them with remaining ¼ pound of butter. Put the purée into a pastry sleeve and squeeze around the edges of the shells or dishes. Sprinkle with red pepper or paprika, and run under the broiler for 5 minutes.

May be assembled and refrigerated in advance; bring to room temperature before baking.

Serves 4

Two-Tiered Tuna Casserole

LEONE C. MCKEEVER
Infirmary

Good old tuna fish—inexpensive and almost always a success for family meals.

4 tablespoons butter

2 small onions, sliced

5 tablespoons chopped green pepper

1½ teaspoons salt

1½ teaspoons pepper

1½ cans cream of mushroom soup

1 package (8 ounces) wide noodles, cooked and drained

1 can (16 ounces) whole tomatoes, drained and roughly chopped

1 can (7 ounces) tuna fish, drained and flaked

¼ teaspoon thyme

1 small package potato chips, crushed

Preheat oven to 400°.

Melt butter, add onions and green pepper, and cook until tender but not browned. Add salt and pepper to the mushroom soup. Butter a 2-quart casserole dish and add layers of half of the following ingredients: noodles, mushroom soup, onions and peppers, tomatoes, tuna fish. Repeat the layers, using the remaining half of the ingredients. Sprinkle the thyme and potato chips on top. Bake for 20 to 25 minutes, uncovered.

Can be assembled well in advance.

Serves 4

Desperation Shrimp

MARGOT FEELY
Publications

For when one has no time and last-minute guests for dinner. The shrimp flavors the sauce as it cooks. Serve with rice or pasta.

24 fresh raw shrimp, shelled and deveined

2 jars (14 ounces each) marinara sauce

1 bay leaf

Oregano or other dried herbs

Chopped parsley

Combine the shrimp with the sauce and dried herbs and bring slowly to a simmer. Cook until the shrimp are done, about ten minutes. Remove bay leaf and sprinkle with parsley.

Serves 4

Conserva

Kedgeree

LINDA GILLIES

Drawings

The English serve this for breakfast; it also makes a good lunch or light supper. Particularly useful if one has leftover fish. Accompany with chutney and serve with a green salad and white wine.

2 cups leftover white fish (sole, bluefish, flounder)

  or a fish that has been poached in white wine,

  water, salt, pepper, and a pinch of thyme

4 cups cooked rice (any kind except instant rice)

1 hard-boiled egg, finely chopped

1½ teaspoons salt

2 teaspoons curry powder

1 tablespoon chopped parsley

Butter or light cream (optional)

1 tablespoon raisins and/or chopped peanuts

  (optional)

Break fish into small bits and mix gently with rest of ingredients. This mixture is quite dry; if a more moist consistency is wanted, add butter or a few tablespoons of cream. Heat thoroughly in a double boiler. Can be prepared well in advance.

Serves 4

Seafood Gumbo

PAMELA PATTERSON
Sales

My husband comes from New Orleans, and this recipe was part of his trousseau. Serve the gumbo with garlic bread.

¼ pound bacon or salt pork, diced
3 tablespoons oil
3 tablespoons flour
2 large onions, minced
2 cups fresh okra, sliced
3 cloves garlic, minced
3 large tomatoes, peeled and chopped
2–3 quarts liquid (water, chicken stock, clam juice, or a combination)
1 bay leaf
2 pounds shrimp, cleaned
6 hard-shell crabs, quartered
1 cup diced ham (optional)
½–1 pound fresh lump crab meat
Salt and pepper
Tabasco sauce
Worcestershire sauce
1 teaspoon filé powder
2 tablespoons parsley
Cooked rice

In a large black cast-iron skillet sauté the bacon or salt pork until transparent. Remove pieces and set aside. In another pan heat 1 tablespoon of the bacon fat with the oil and stir in the flour to make a roux. To the remaining bacon fat add the onion, okra, and garlic, and sauté until golden. Add the tomatoes and cook until the liquid has been absorbed. Add the roux and stir in liquid and bay leaf. Bring to a low simmer for 30 minutes. Add the shrimp and hard-shell crabs and simmer for 30 minutes. Stir in the reserved bacon or salt pork pieces, ham, crab meat, salt and pepper to taste, Tabasco, and Worcestershire. Simmer until thoroughly heated. If too thick, adjust with extra liquid. Stir in filé powder and sprinkle with parsley before serving in a deep bowl over a scoop of rice.

Serves 6 to 8

ghiottela

Never-Fail Béarnaise Sauce

BRADFORD KELLEHER
Publications

White wine is used in the classic French version, but the vermouth gives a somewhat richer taste. When doubling the recipe, do not quite double the shallots and tarragon.

1 generous teaspoon dried tarragon
1 generous teaspoon chopped shallots
Salt and pepper
4 tablespoons wine vinegar
⅓ cup dry vermouth
2 egg yolks, mixed with 1 teaspoon water
¼ pound sweet butter

Place tarragon, shallots, salt and pepper to taste, vinegar, and vermouth in a small saucepan and bring to boil, reducing to two-thirds of original volume. Bring water to a boil in the bottom half of a double boiler. Strain tarragon mixture into the *cool* top half of the double boiler and place pot over (but not touching) water, which should be kept at a slow, steady boil. Gradually stir in the eggs with a wire whisk. Stirring steadily, add the butter, tablespoon by tablespoon, allowing each to melt before adding the next. When all the butter is used and the sauce has become thick enough, put top half of double boiler into a pan of cold water for a few minutes to stop the cooking.

Serves 4

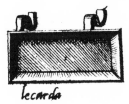

lecarda

85

Betsy Marden's Hollandaise Mustard

LINDA GILLIES
Drawings

From a former neighbor, who used to give jars of this strong mustard sauce as Christmas presents, and even sold it commercially.

3–4 egg yolks (depending on size)
1 cup sugar
1 cup dry mustard
2 cups cider vinegar
Butter the size of an egg

Beat the egg yolks with the sugar and add the dry mustard. Stir in the vinegar and cook over the lowest possible heat or in a double boiler, stirring, until it coats the spoon. Add the butter and cool, stirring occasionally. The sauce will thicken slightly as it cools.

Will keep for a long time in the refrigerator.

Approximately 3 cups

Vegetables, Salads, & Salad Dressings

Ruota del Conclaue

Mazziere

di Cocina

Tauola, doue li Scalchi presentano le uiuande delli Rmi, Alli reueditori.

Scala di ritorno

Red Cabbage

LINDA GILLIES
Drawings

This recipe is from Janos Scholz, a member of the Visiting Committee to the Drawings Department. It originates in Sopron, Hungary, and has been in his family since about 1800. To be served with pheasant, venison, ham, and pork but never, says Mr. Scholz, with partridge or grouse!

3 ounces double-smoked Hungarian bacon, cut in small pieces
1 large onion, chopped
2 firm heads red cabbage, shredded
2 cloves garlic, minced
1 tablespoon caraway seeds
Salt and small amount ground pepper
2 large pears, peeled, cored, and chopped
1 lemon, halved
3 glasses red wine
3 tablespoons fine wine vinegar
1 cup honey
Brown sugar (if necessary)

Coltelli maestri da battere

Brown the pieces of bacon in a large cast-iron pot until golden brown. Add the chopped onion and simmer, uncovered, until onion starts to turn blond. Add the cabbage, garlic, caraway seeds, and 1 cup of boiling water. Cover and cook until cabbage starts to get limp. Add salt, pepper, pears, lemon, red wine, and vinegar. Cover and cook for about 10 minutes. Only then add the honey and continue to cook, covered, over a very low heat. If after 30 minutes there is too much liquid, remove the cover and let half of it steam away. Only about 1 inch of liquid should remain. At this point taste the cabbage. If it is not sour-sweet enough, add brown sugar to taste. Remove the pieces of lemon. Continue cooking slowly until the cabbage is reduced to less than half its original amount, approximately 30 minutes. The pears should have completely disappeared. Add salt if necessary, but very judiciously. Keep warm, with the cover slightly off, until serving.

Like so many Hungarian dishes, it is advisable to prepare the cabbage a day in advance.

Serves 4

Purée of Corn

PAGE AYRES
Drawings

Especially good with roasted or grilled meat.

2 cans (12 ounces each) white shoe peg corn
Salt and pepper

Blend corn, one can at a time, in electric blender. It should be about the consistency of mashed potatoes. Heat in the top of a double boiler and season to taste.

Serves 4

Crinello

French Fried Eggplant

PAMELA PATTERSON
Sales

The eggplants in my garden went rampant one year. This was one of the most successful solutions for what to do with them.

2 eggs, beaten
1 tablespoon oregano
1 eggplant, peeled and cut into thumb-sized pieces
Bread crumbs
Vegetable oil
Salt and pepper

Mix the eggs, ¼ cup water, and oregano. Dip the eggplant pieces in the mixture. Shake the pieces in a bag filled with bread crumbs, then lay them on a cookie sheet for 10 minutes. Fry in 1½ inches of oil, turning and shaking constantly until golden brown, 5 to 7 minutes. Season. Can be kept warm for a while, but best if served right away.

Serves 4 to 6

Endives in Cream

JACOB BEAN
Drawings

The two cheeses, which melt in the cream, produce a delicious sauce. Serve as a first course or with roasted or grilled meat.

> 8 small or medium Belgian endives
> ½ cup finely grated fresh Parmesan cheese
> 1½ cups coarsely grated imported Gruyère cheese
> Freshly ground pepper and salt
> 2 cups heavy cream

Preheat oven to 375°.

Steam the endives until tender, about 10 minutes. Place in a single layer in a baking dish just large enough to hold them. Sprinkle on the cheeses, pepper, and salt (not too much, as the Parmesan is salty to begin with). Cover the endives and cheeses with cream. Bake at the top of the oven until browned, about 30 minutes.

   The dish may be assembled in advance and refrigerated. Bring to room temperature before baking.

Serves 4

Conserva

Endive Casserole

DAVID TURPIN
Library

May be served as an individual course or as an accompanying vegetable. Good reheated.

> 8 small Belgian endives
> 8 slices precooked ham
> 1 can cream of mushroom soup
> 1 cup (½ pint) sour cream
> 4–6 tablespoons butter
> 1 tablespoon cognac (optional)
> ½ pound mushrooms, sliced
> 6–8 ounces imported Gruyère cheese, cut into
>   julienne strips

Ostreghine

Preheat oven to 375°.

Steam the endives in a steamer or small amount of water for about 10 minutes, until just tender. Squeeze them out and wrap each piece in a slice of ham, securing with a couple of toothpicks. Place four pieces in a well-buttered 3-quart casserole dish. Warm the soup, sour cream, butter, and cognac in a small saucepan (do not boil). Spoon half this sauce over the layer of endive. Sprinkle half the mushrooms over the endive and add half the cheese strips. Repeat successive layers of endives, mushrooms, sauce, and cheese, in that order. Cover and bake for 50 minutes; uncover and bake for 15 minutes, until brown on top.

Serves **4** as a course, **6 to 8** as a vegetable

Okra Creole

EDITH CULLEN
Drawings

From Dean Walker, a former graduate intern in the department. The recipe has been passed to members of his family for at least three generations, but has not been written down until now.

3 tablespoons bacon fat (or more, for a stronger
 bacon flavor)
1 medium onion, chopped
1½ pounds fresh okra, or 2 packages (10 ounces
 each) frozen whole okra (more tender than the
 sliced), sliced into ½–1-inch pieces
1 can (16 ounces) tomatoes (with juice), or an
 equivalent amount of fresh, peeled and cut into
 bite-size pieces
1 can (8 ounces) tomato sauce (optional, for a
 stronger tomato flavor)
1 teaspoon salt
¼ teaspoon pepper
Cooked bacon, crumbled (optional)

Heat the bacon fat in a skillet or saucepan and sauté the onions until tender. Add the remaining ingredients and cook over a low heat, covered, until the juice is absorbed, about 30 minutes. Sprinkle with bacon if you wish.

Serves 4

Spinach Revisited

DONNA C. SMIDT
Photograph and Slide Library

This recipe may be varied by adding crumbled crisp bacon or sautéed mushrooms to the spinach mixture.

Infator ouato

> 1 small or medium onion, chopped
> Butter
> 1 package (3 ounces) cream cheese, softened
> 1 package frozen chopped spinach, thawed and drained
> 1 egg, beaten
> ¼ cup bread crumbs or fine prepared stuffing (not cubed)
> Salt and pepper
> Paprika

Preheat oven to 350°.

Sauté the onion in 2 tablespoons of butter until transparent. In a bowl mash the cream cheese with a fork. Add the onion, spinach, egg, bread crumbs, and salt and pepper to taste. Pour into a small buttered casserole, sprinkle with paprika, and dot with butter. Bake, uncovered, for 20 minutes.

May be assembled and refrigerated in advance; bring to room temperature before baking.

Serves 3 to 4

String Bean Casserole

MRS. RICHARD SILBERSTEIN
Trustee

Useful for school dinners and such, as it's easy to make in large quantities, inexpensive, and doesn't spoil easily.

2 packages frozen string beans
1 can cream of mushroom soup
¾ pound mushrooms, sliced
1 cup grated cheddar cheese
1 can (3 ounces) onion rings, crumbled
Paprika

Preheat oven to 350°.

Cook the string beans until slightly underdone. Fill a casserole to top with the following layers: mushroom soup, beans, sliced mushrooms, cheese, onion rings. Sprinkle the top layer with paprika, adding a few mushroom caps if you wish. Heat in oven for 20 minutes, or until cheese melts and the casserole is brown on top.

Serves 4 to 6

Sweet Potato Soufflé

ANITA MULLER
Sales

Something new for Thanksgiving lunch.

3–4 sweet potatoes (depending on size)
¾ cup hot milk
3 tablespoons butter
1 teaspoon salt
¼ teaspoon allspice
¼ teaspoon ground cardamom seed
2 eggs, separated
2 tablespoons sugar

Preheat oven to 350°.

Peel sweet potatoes, cut into 2-inch chunks, and boil for 20 minutes, or until tender. Drain and mash with a fork. Combine potatoes, milk, butter, salt, allspice, and cardamom. Beat the egg yolks into this mixture. Beat the egg whites until they stand in peaks, gradually adding the sugar. Fold carefully into the sweet potatoes. Turn into a buttered soufflé dish and bake until firm in center, about 1 hour. Serve immediately.

Serves 4

93

Zucchini and Rice

PHYLLIS DEARBORN MASSAR
Prints and Photographs

I usually return from trips to Italy with a new recipe or two—they seem to adapt to American ingredients more easily than French ones. This one comes from a friend in Lucca who, when he found he had no peas to make *risi e bisi*, substituted zucchini. Serve as a first course or as an accompaniment to a meat course.

> ⅓ cup raw rice per person
> 1 medium zucchini for every two persons
> Salt
> 1 thin slice boiled ham, diced, per person
> Butter to taste
> About ⅛ cup freshly grated Parmesan cheese
> per person

Cook the rice as usual and keep warm, preferably in a steamer. Meanwhile, halve each zucchini lengthwise and then slice crosswise into fairly thin pieces. Cook in a fair amount of water and salt until just tender; drain. Combine all the ingredients.

Grated Zucchini

ANITA MULLER
Sales

One of the nicest ways to serve zucchini.

> 6 small zucchini
> Salt
> 4 tablespoons butter (or more)
> Freshly ground pepper
> Parsley or other herbs in season, finely chopped

Grate the zucchini on the coarse side of the grater, salt it, and place in a colander lined with paper towels. Let stand for 20 minutes, until the excess liquid has been absorbed. Remove the paper towels and rinse the zucchini well. Squeeze it with your fingers and pat with paper towels. Melt the butter in a large skillet, add the dry zucchini, pepper, and herbs, and sauté until soft and slightly golden (about 15 minutes). Add more butter if it seems necessary.

Serves 4

Chili Rellenos Casserole

WESTON NAEF
Prints and Photographs

Adapted by Mary Naef from a recipe originally in the *Los Angeles Times*. Simple, inexpensive, and tasty. Serve with tacos.

BEAN MIXTURE
- 2 cans (15 ounces each) refried beans (or 2 cans kidney beans, drained and mashed; cook until thick in 2 tablespoons oil with 1 teaspoon chili powder and ½ teaspoon minced garlic)
- 2 cans (4 ounces each) green chili peppers, chopped
- ½–1 pound cheese (Monterey Jack or ½ Muenster, ½ mild cheddar), cut into ½-inch cubes
- 4 eggs, separated
- 3–4 tablespoons flour
- 1 teaspoon baking powder

SAUCE
- 1 can (10 ounces) green chili salsa or tomatoes and green chilies
- ¼–½ cup chicken broth
- 1 teaspoon oregano

Preheat oven to 350°.

Place the beans on the bottom of a greased two-quart casserole. Add half the peppers, the cheese, and the remaining peppers in layers. Beat the egg whites until firm. Beat the yolks and add them to the whites. Mix in the flour and baking powder. Spread on top of the bean mixture, and bake for 30 to 40 minutes, until slightly browned. In the meantime, combine the ingredients for the sauce and simmer for 15 minutes. Serve warm with the casserole.

Serves 4

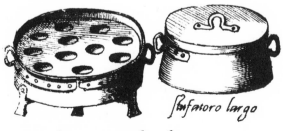

padella p̃ fare oui frittolate   *stufatoro largo*

Stuffed Mixed Vegetables

BERTHA RICHIE
Sales

A great recipe for anyone with a vegetable garden.

3 tomatoes

2 zucchini

2 eggplants

3 green peppers

1 medium onion, chopped

2 tablespoons butter

1 small clove garlic, minced

Oregano

Basil (fresh, if possible)

2 cups minced leftover meat (or 1 pound chopped meat, browned)

1 egg

Approximately 2 cups tomato sauce, fresh or canned

Preheat oven to 375°.

Cut the tomatoes, zucchini, eggplants, and peppers in half and scoop out the pulp, being careful to keep the outer parts intact. Chop the pulp and set aside. Steam the green pepper and zucchini until just tender. Sauté the onion in the butter until transparent, and add the garlic, vegetable pulp, and herbs to taste. Mix in the meat and egg. Fill the vegetable shells with the mixture, place them in a shallow baking dish, and cover each with a layer of tomato sauce. Bake until the pepper is cooked, about 30 minutes. If the vegetables appear to be getting dry, add a little water.

Serves 6

Cole Slaw

ANITA MULLER
Sales

gratta caſſio

Almost always a hit with children.

> 1 large head cabbage
> ½ cup sour cream
> ½ cup vinegar
> 1 cup mayonnaise
> 1 teaspoon sugar
> 1 teaspoon dried dill
> 1 diced apple
> Salt and pepper

Shred cabbage into a large bowl. Mix in other ingredients, cover, and marinate for 2 to 3 hours in the refrigerator.

Serves 6

Sweet and Sour Salad

JULIE LEONARD
American Wing

Add other vegetables if you wish—tomatoes, raw carrots, cucumber, parsley.

> 1 large head iceberg lettuce
> 1 cup salad oil
> ¼ – ½ cup cider vinegar
> Sugar to taste
> 1½ cups dry crouton stuffing
> Red onions, thinly sliced

Prepare the lettuce. Combine the oil, vinegar, and sugar, and toss with the lettuce, stuffing, and onions just before serving.

Serves 6

Endive Salad

COLTA IVES
Prints and Photographs

The idea is from a small restaurant on the Île St.-Louis in Paris, where, with a Museum travel grant, I was doing research on Toulouse-Lautrec.

4 heads Belgian endive
1 bunch watercress (sprigs snipped from top of
  bunch)
1 can (4 ounces) walnuts, roughly chopped
2 tablespoons vegetable oil
2 tablespoons olive oil
1 tablespoon wine vinegar
1 tablespoon lemon juice
¼ teaspoon salt
Pinch dry mustard

Crisp the endive and watercress in a bowl of ice water for 10 to 15 minutes. Dry well with paper towels. Slice endive heads lengthwise, then across two or three times. Combine with watercress and walnuts. Refrigerate.

Shake the remaining ingredients for the dressing vigorously in a jar. Just before serving toss with the salad so as to coat the greens lightly.

Serves 4 to 6

navicella bassa

Esau's Mess of Pottage

CARELLA ALDEN
Membership

Served at a cast party given by Mrs. Thomas O. Mabbott for staff members who were in one of the Museum's Art Entertainments. Surround with raw vegetables—tomatoes, carrots, cucumber, or what you will. For a nice variation, mix the salad with vinaigrette dressing.

1 cup lentils

1 tablespoon salt

¾ cup raw long-grain rice

6 medium onions, sliced or chopped

¾ cup olive oil

Salt and freshly ground pepper

Chopped parsley

Cook the lentils in 7 cups of salted water for 30 minutes. Add the rice and cook for another 15 minutes. Drain. In the meantime, sauté the onions in oil over low heat, covered, until they are transparent but not browned. Combine the lentil mixture and onions and refrigerate. Correct seasoning and sprinkle with parsley.

Serves 6 to 8

Curried Chicken Salad

PAMELA PATTERSON
Sales

You may also add cucumbers, raisins, or whatever else strikes your fancy.

1 chicken, poached and cut into bite-size pieces

1 teaspoon salt

Freshly ground pepper

1 cup mayonnaise

Juice of 1 lemon

1 tablespoon curry powder (to taste)

1 small jar Major Grey's chutney, drained and chopped

¼ cup finely chopped scallions

½ cup roughly chopped toasted almonds

Finely chopped parsley

Combine all ingredients in the order given, mix, and sprinkle with parsley.

Serves 6

Mary Murphy's Green Salad Dressing

MRS. CHARLES S. PAYSON
Trustee

Menu for a Saturday lunch: cold Senegalese soup, cheese soufflé, and tomato and lettuce salad with green salad dressing.

½ cup roughly chopped parsley (no stems)
½ cup roughly chopped watercress (no stems)
8 shallot cloves, peeled
1 teaspoon Accent
1 teaspoon dry mustard
1 teaspoon Worcestershire sauce
½ cup tarragon vinegar
½ cup safflower oil
3 egg yolks
1 teaspoon salt
1 teaspoon horseradish
¼ cup ice water

Blend all ingredients together in blender. If too thick add a few tablespoons of ice water.

Crinello

Tarragon Salad Dressing

CHEF MARIO
Restaurant

While working as an assistant chef at the Tower Suite Restaurant in New York, Mario found himself in a predicament—the chef was away and the restaurant had run out of salad dressing. Quickly Mario took what ingredients were at hand and invented this dressing, which subsequently became a Tower Suite favorite.

1 jar (12 ounces) tarragon leaves
1 bottle (5 ounces) Worcestershire sauce
1 teaspoon Tabasco sauce
1 teaspoon freshly ground white pepper
1 tablespoon salt
2 sprigs parsley
1 medium onion, finely chopped
½ cup red wine vinegar
2 cups vegetable oil
1 cup chicken consommé
2½ pounds mayonnaise

Place all ingredients except the oil, consommé, and mayonnaise in a blender and mix at high speed. Empty into a bowl. Slowly mix in the consommé and oil. When the mixture reaches the consistency of a loose purée, add the mayonnaise a little at a time, beating constantly with a wire whisk. Chill and serve.

2 quarts

Three Low-Calorie Salad Dressings

LOUISE CONDIT
Junior Museum

My husband, Frederic G. M. Lange, is a passionate cook, and credit for these and the recipe for spaghetti sauce (page 112) goes to him.

BASIC ⅓ cup plus 1 tablespoon sugar
RECIPE 1 tablespoon salt
¾ cup cider vinegar
⅔ cup cold water

Variation 1 (for cucumbers, meat and fish salads, deviled eggs): add 1 teaspoon dill seeds, pulverized with mortar and pestle

Variation 2 (for avocado, cucumbers, tomatoes): add ½ teaspoon fennel and ½ teaspoon anise, pulverized with mortar and pestle

Variation 3 (for green salad, hot potato salad, string bean salad): add ¼ cup ketchup, oil to taste

Shake ingredients well, and refrigerate for several days.

Noodles, Rice, Pasta, & Their Sauces

Noodle Casserole

PAMELA PATTERSON
Sales

ghiottela

Excellent with veal or any roast.

> 1 box (12 ounces) *fine* noodles
> Butter
> 1 medium onion, minced
> 1 clove garlic, minced
> 1 tablespoon Worcestershire sauce
> 1 teaspoon salt
> 1 teaspoon freshly ground pepper
> 1 pound creamed cottage cheese
> 3 cups (1½ pints) sour cream (more for serving if wished)
> Grated Parmesan cheese

Preheat oven to 350°.

Cook noodles in rapidly boiling water for about 10 minutes until tender, drain, and put into buttered casserole. Meanwhile, melt ¼ pound butter in a skillet and sauté onion and garlic until transparent. Turn heat off and blend in Worcestershire, salt, pepper, cottage cheese, and 3 cups sour cream. Combine mixture with noodles, sprinkle with Parmesan cheese, and dot with butter. Cover and bake 45 minutes, then uncover and bake 15 minutes. Serve with extra sour cream and Parmesan cheese if desired.

  This can be assembled in advance and refrigerated. Make sure that it is room temperature before baking.

Serves 8

Korean-Style Rice

ANITA KOH
Ancient Near Eastern Art

At a Korean meal each person usually has a covered metal rice bowl at his place. Unlike the Chinese and Japanese, Koreans eat rice with a spoon. While the rice cooks you may add small amounts of any of the following: precooked red beans, mung beans, chestnuts, or uncooked green peas. Or use your imagination.

½ cup medium-grain rice per person, washed until
water runs clear

Place rice in a large pan and cover with water so that the level comes above rice to the first joint of your finger. Let sit 30 minutes. Cook, covered, over high heat for 10 minutes or so until boiling furiously. Turn to very low heat and cook 15 to 20 minutes. Turn off heat and let rice sit for 10 to 15 minutes before serving. Do not remove cover at any point, or the steam will escape and the rice will not cook properly.

Green Rice Ring

MRS. SHELDON WHITEHOUSE
Trustee

These colorful and delicious molds can be filled with creamed chicken or crab meat, sautéed mushrooms, carrots, and so on.

namicella alta

2 cups cooked rice
1 bunch scallions, finely chopped
½ cup finely chopped parsley
½ cup finely chopped celery
3 eggs, separated
½ cup heavy cream
½ cup butter
Salt and pepper
Dry bread crumbs

Preheat oven to 450°.

Combine rice, scallions, parsley, celery, egg yolks, cream, ½ cup melted butter, and salt and pepper to taste. Beat the egg whites until stiff and fold gently into the rice mixture. Butter a ring mold generously and coat it with bread crumbs. Pour in the rice mixture and place in a shallow pan of water. Bake for about 45 minutes, or until set. Turn out onto a round platter.

Serves 4

Molded Green Rice

PAMELA PATTERSON
Sales

¾ cup butter
½ cup chicken stock
1 bunch scallions, chopped
1 bunch parsley, chopped
Salt and pepper
6 cups cooked rice

Preheat oven to 350°.

Melt butter in chicken stock, then put all ingredients except rice in a blender. Blend until they are bright, pistachiolike green. In a bowl, mix rice with blended mixture. Spoon into a buttered mold, cover with foil, and place in a roasting pan containing 1 inch water. Bake for 20 to 25 minutes. Unmold, fill, and serve.

Serves 10 to 12

Three Ways to Cook Brown Rice

HENRY GELDZAHLER
Twentieth-Century Art

The organically grown brown rice available at most health food stores is of much higher quality than supermarket brown rice, which (although far superior to white rice) has probably been grown with chemical fertilizers and sprayed with insecticides. Just as we value the quality of handmade works of art, we must learn to place greater value and pay a higher price for food that is grown by hand.

There are many different kinds of rice, but they are usually divided into three basic categories: long, medium, and short grain. Short-grain rice has a rugged look about it and is usually more glutinous than long-grain, which is lighter and more delicate. Ask yourself, "Which one do I need? Which one is best for us today?"

With works of art we consider value as well as quality. Picasso and Matisse, for instance, are painters whose best works are of equally high quality. Yet, at various times we prefer one to the other; our intuition tells us that at the moment we need it more. Just so, a meal cannot be composed of all the good foods that are available at any given time. The good cook must sense what he, his family, and his guests need to make their body chemistry appropriate for the locale and for the moment, the seasons, and the age.

Pressure-cooked Rice. Orientals like rice that is sweet and gummy. A nonelectric pressure cooker makes this kind of rice best. Don't shy away from pressure-cooked rice because you prefer fluffy rice. When Westerners cook white rice and it comes out gummy, the meal may indeed be a partial failure. But pressure-cooked brown rice has a delicious flavor that is worth a try.

Brown rice often needs to be washed well. Place 1 cup of rice in a pressure cooker. Cover rice with water and stir. Drain cloudy water and repeat process until water is clear.

Pour 1¾ cups spring water over clean rice in pressure cooker. Add ¼ teaspoon sea salt (more in winter, less in summer). Pressure-cook for 45 minutes at a temperature just high enough to keep the little what-cha-ma-call-it on top of the cooker rattling.

Boiled Rice. Boiled brown rice can turn out relatively fluffy or porridgey, depending on how much water you use. Generally 2½ cups water to 1 cup rice is the ideal ration. Use a heavy cast-iron pot, enameled or plain, that has a good lid. Wash rice as above. Add water. Boil for 10 minutes with lid off. Skim off scum. Add ¼ teaspoon salt and cover. Simmer for 45 minutes, without lifting cover.

Fluffy Rice. Pour 1 tablespoon of vegetable oil (preferably cold pressed and unrefined) into a preheated cast-iron skillet. Sauté a cup of rice over a low flame for about 20 minutes, until golden brown. In the meantime bring 1½ cups water and ¼ teaspoon salt to a rolling boil and then to a simmer. Slowly add the hot rice, being careful the resulting explosion does not cause the rice to overflow. Cover and simmer for 30 minutes.

Thanks for this recipe go to Christopher Scott.

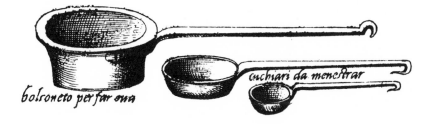

bolsoneto per far oua   cuchiari da menestrar

Spaghetti with Tomato and Basil Sauce

THOMAS HOVING
Director

While living in Rome my wife and I often feasted on pasta served with tomatoes and lots of fresh basil, the specialty of a neighborhood trattoria. We have spent years trying to duplicate the sauce, and think we have by now come pretty close.

2 medium or large cloves garlic, finely chopped
6 large tomatoes, seeded and cut into bite-size pieces
24 large fresh basil leaves, torn into small pieces
Salt and pepper
¼ – ½ cup olive oil
1½ pounds spaghetti

Combine all ingredients except spaghetti and let stand in a warm spot for an hour or more. Cook and drain the spaghetti. Pour it into the tomato mixture, toss, and serve.

Serves 6

Spaghettini with Sausage and Zucchini

JAMES DELIHAS
Public Affairs

The beauty of this superlative recipe is its flexibility. Almost any vegetable or a combination thereof may be substituted for the zucchini and mushrooms—sliced string beans, cubed eggplant, diced new potatoes, peas, or fennel. For a vegetarian dish, eliminate the sausages. With the exception of the pasta, the dish may be prepared in advance and reheated.

½ cup olive oil
2 large onions, chopped
2 cloves garlic, minced
1 small carrot, sliced in rounds
1 small stalk celery, chopped

foratoro colmanico

2 jars (14 ounces each) plain spaghetti sauce
   (Aunt Millie's is good)
1 bay leaf, crumbled
Oregano
Thyme
Pinch sugar (if needed)
1½ pounds Italian sausage, half sweet, half hot,
   sliced in rounds
½ pound mushrooms, sliced
1 pound small zucchini, sliced on the diagonal into
   ½-inch pieces
1 pound spaghettini
Freshly grated Parmesan cheese

Heat ¼ cup of the oil in a heavy casserole and sauté the onions, garlic, carrot, and celery until limp. Add the spaghetti sauce and herbs and sugar to taste, bring to a boil, cover, and simmer until the vegetables are tender, about 20 minutes. Meanwhile, in a small skillet heat the remaining ¼ cup olive oil and brown the sausages in it, stirring until cooked through, about 10 minutes. Add the mushrooms and zucchini and cook, stirring, until lightly browned. With a slotted spoon transfer the sausages, mushrooms, and zucchini to the casserole in which the sauce is cooking, and simmer gently until the zucchini is just cooked, about 10 minutes. Meanwhile cook the spaghettini *al dente* and drain. Pour the sauce over it and top with lots of Parmesan cheese.

Serves 6

Rigatoni alla Panna
(rigatoni with cream sauce)

DANNY BERGER
Sales

Danny Berger sent this wonderful recipe from Rome, where he now lives and does some work for the Museum. If rigatoni is not available, other types of pasta may be used.

pignatta grande

8 ounces rigatoni

Salt

Bay leaf

2 tablespoons butter

¼ teaspoon dry English mustard

½ pint heavy cream

2 egg yolks

½ cup grated Parmesan cheese (it *must* be fresh)

Salt and freshly ground pepper

Cook the pasta *al dente* in salted water to which you have added a bay leaf. While it cooks prepare the sauce.

Melt the butter over a low-medium heat and add the mustard, stirring with a wire whisk until smooth. Add the cream and beat in the egg yolks, one at a time. Stirring continuously, slowly add the cheese until the sauce thickens enough to coat the side of the pan. Do not let the sauce boil. Add a little salt and pepper.

Drain the pasta, place it in a warm serving dish, and pour the hot sauce over it. Serve immediately.

Serves 4

Pasta with Mushrooms and Cream

JOHN HOWAT
American Paintings and Sculpture

If you want to live very well, substitute minced truffles (with the liquid if canned) for the mushrooms in this recipe.

1 small onion, minced

1 small clove garlic, minced

3 tablespoons butter

1 cup mushrooms, minced or sliced

1 cup heavy cream

Salt and pepper

8 ounces pasta shells or quills

⅓ – ½ cup freshly grated Parmesan cheese

110

In a covered pan, sauté the onion and garlic in butter until transparent. Add the mushrooms and stir, uncovered, for 2 minutes. Add the cream and salt and pepper to taste, and stir the mixture over a high heat until it thickens.

In the meantime, cook the pasta in salted water. Drain, mix with the sauce, and toss in the grated Parmesan at the last minute.

Serves 4

Fettucine with Mushrooms

LINDA GILLIES
Drawings

In Rome I watched the famous Alfredo make platter after platter of perfect fettucine and tried to discover his secret. Rather than pouring the cream and cheese on top of cooked pasta, he placed these and other ingredients in the dish before adding the pasta. The cheese melted as it mixed from the bottom of the pan through the hot noodles and produced a creamy sauce—not grainy, as mine so often had been.

foratoro

> Freshly grated Parmesan cheese
> ⅔ cup heavy cream
> 5 tablespoons butter
> Salt
> Freshly ground pepper
> 12 ounces fettucine
> ½ pound mushrooms, sliced (don't wash them—
>   they absorb the water and lose their taste)
> A squeeze of lemon juice

Place ½ cup of cheese, cream, 3 tablespoons of butter, 1 teaspoon of salt, and pepper to taste in a platter and keep warm—you want the cream to warm slightly and the butter to start to melt. Do not let the platter get too hot, or the cheese will start to melt—disaster. Cook the pasta *al dente*. Meanwhile sauté the mushrooms rapidly in 2 tablespoons of butter and add lemon juice. When they are limp sprinkle with salt. Drain the pasta and place on top of ingredients in the platter. Add the mushrooms and mix all quickly and thoroughly. Serve immediately with additional grated Parmesan.

Serves 4

"World's Best Spaghetti Sauce"

LOUISE CONDIT
Junior Museum

The fruits and vegetables give this sauce a rather sweet, unusual flavor. It should be served on spaghetti cooked *al dente* and sprinkled with grated Parmesan and Romano cheeses. Accompany with green salad and a Chianti.

1 tablespoon olive oil	3 black olives, thinly sliced
1 small clove garlic, finely chopped or pressed	1 teaspoon dried currants
	1 teaspoon seedless raisins
1 pound ground beef	1 small green pepper, sliced
½ cup ketchup	½ roasted pepper or pimento, sliced
½ cup hot ketchup	2 ounces mushrooms, sliced
½ cup chili sauce	Pinch Italian red pepper (optional)
1 tablespoon oregano	1½ tablespoons pine nuts
3 green olives, thinly sliced	4 slices mozzarella cheese

In a heavy pan heat the olive oil and brown the garlic. Add the meat, break it up with a fork, and brown. Add the ketchups, chili sauce, ½ cup water, oregano, and olives. Stir well and simmer slowly (use flame retarder if you have one) for at least 25 minutes. Add the currants and raisins, and simmer 5 minutes. If sauce becomes too thick, add a small quantity of boiling water. Add the green pepper and roasted pepper or pimento, and keep simmering very slowly. When the peppers are nearly done, add the mushrooms. Stir gently. Sprinkle with red pepper if desired, and stir in pine nuts. Cover and cool.

Before serving reheat slowly, stirring occasionally. Taste and correct seasoning. When sauce is hot, add the mozzarella cheese, stirring constantly thereafter to avoid sticking. Serve as soon as cheese has melted.

3 cups

Quiches, Soufflés, & Eggs

Quiche Lorraine

CHRISTINE ROUSSEL
Sculpture Reproduction Workshop

The onions and sour cream give a pungent taste to this variation on the classic quiche.

> 4–6 strips of bacon, cut into ½-inch pieces
> 1 small or medium onion, chopped
> 1 clove garlic, minced
> 1½ cups grated imported Gruyère cheese
> ¼ cup grated Parmesan cheese
> 4 eggs, lightly beaten
> 2 cups (1 pint) sour cream, thinned with ¼ cup milk
> ¼ teaspoon nutmeg
> Salt and pepper
> A 9-inch pie shell, partially baked

Preheat oven to 450°.

Fry the bacon until crisp. Remove and drain, leaving fat in pan. Sauté the onion and garlic in the bacon fat until transparent, drain, and mix in bacon. Combine cheeses, eggs, sour cream, nutmeg, and salt and pepper to taste. Spread half the bacon-onion mixture in the bottom of the pie shell, pour in the cheese mixture, and add the remaining bacon. Reduce oven to 350° and bake pie 30 to 35 minutes, until a knife inserted into the custard comes out clean. Set aside for several hours (it is even better the next day), and reheat at 350° for about 20 minutes before serving.

Serves 6

Coperchi per tortere

Tiropeta
(Greek cheese pie)

NORA ORPHANIDES
Sales

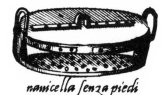

namicella senza piedi

The Greek version of quiche.

> 12 eggs
> 1 pound feta cheese
> 1 pound ricotta cheese
> 1 pound butter, melted and cooled
> ½ pound phyllo pastry sheets (available at any
>   Greek bakery)

Preheat oven to 350°.

Beat the eggs until thick. In another bowl mix the cheeses with half the melted butter; add the eggs. Thoroughly coat the phyllo sheets with the remaining butter and line a baking pan (11 by 14 by 2 inches) with half of them. Pour in the cheese mixture and cover with the remaining phyllo sheets. Tuck the pastry in around the sides of the pan so all is firm and neat. Bake for about 30 minutes, until golden brown. Cut in squares and serve warm.

16 squares

Lettuce and Bacon Quiche

SISI CAHAN
Development and Promotion

Especially useful if you have too much lettuce in the garden.

> 4 large heads of lettuce (romaine, escarole,
>   chicory, or a combination)
> 1 medium onion, finely chopped
> 3 tablespoons butter
> 1 cup heavy or light cream
> 2 eggs, beaten
> ½ teaspoon salt (or more, to taste)
> ½ teaspoon pepper
> 1 pound bacon, fried until crisp, and crumbled
> A 9-inch pie shell, partially baked
> Freshly grated Parmesan cheese
> Bread crumbs

Cucumo

Preheat oven to 375°.

Steam lettuce until tender, drain well, and chop very finely. Sauté the onion in 2 tablespoons of the butter until transparent and add to the greens. Stir the cream into the eggs until just mixed, add salt, pepper, and bacon, and combine mixture with greens. Pour into the pastry shell, sprinkle with cheese and bread crumbs, and dot with remaining tablespoon of butter. Bake for 30 minutes.

The greens mixture may be prepared in advance, but should be poured into the pastry shell and cooked just before serving.

Serves 6

Cheese Soufflé

KATHARINE STODDERT
Bulletin and Calendar/News

If you have an electric oven don't forget to remove the top coil; the heat should come from below.

1 teaspoon grated onion or onion flakes

¼ teaspoon minced celery tops or celery flakes

¼ teaspoon salt

¼ teaspoon dry mustard

¼ teaspoon marjoram

¼ teaspoon brandy extract

⅛ teaspoon pepper

1 bay leaf

Pinch nutmeg

½ cup milk

2 tablespoons butter

2 tablespoons flour

½ pound sharp cheddar cheese, grated

3 egg yolks, at room temperature

4 egg whites, at room temperature, with pinch of salt

Preheat oven to 375°.

Simmer the first 9 ingredients in the milk for about 5 minutes over very low heat, so they steep but do not boil. The mixture can then be strained if you prefer a perfectly smooth soufflé (remove the bay leaf in any case). Melt the butter in the seasoned milk. Sprinkle in flour, stirring constantly until smooth and thickened. Add the grated cheese, stirring until it melts. Remove from heat. Beat the egg yolks until pale. In a separate bowl beat the whites until stiff. Add the yolks to the cheese mixture, stirring thoroughly. Gently fold in half the whites, and then add the rest. Pour into an ungreased 6-inch soufflé dish, and bake in a pan containing ½ inch hot water for 30 to 45 minutes, depending on your oven.

Serves 2

Western European Arts Omelet

CLARE VINCENT
Western European Arts

A recipe from a former member of the WEA staff, who in turn learned it from another member of the department. It is especially nice for Sunday brunch, but with a bottle of dry white wine and a salad will do for a light supper.

> 3 cloves garlic (to taste; omit completely if you
>   wish), sliced
> 2 tablespoons butter
> 4 eggs
> ¼ teaspoon chives
> ½ teaspoon chopped parsley
> Salt and pepper
> 3 tablespoons cream cheese, cut into ½-inch
>   chunks

gratta cassio

This omelet is most easily done in a Teflon pan. Wilt the garlic in butter over a medium heat. Beat the eggs and 1 teaspoon of water with a wire whisk until they are foamy. Add the chives, parsley, and salt and pepper to taste, and pour into the frying pan with the garlic. Stir with a fork until the garlic is mixed in and the eggs begin to hold together. Then sprinkle the chunks of cream cheese over the top and cook for a few minutes longer. The omelet is done when the eggs are still slightly runny and the cream cheese has just begun to melt. Fold one side over the other and carefully slide the omelet onto a heated serving dish. Serve immediately.

Serves 2

Curried Eggs

EDWARD M. M. WARBURG
Vice-Director for Public Affairs

For a light lunch or a Sunday night supper.

6 tablespoons butter
6 tablespoons flour
2 ¼ cups milk
1 ½ teaspoons salt
¾ teaspoon pepper
2–3 teaspoons curry powder (to taste)
8 eggs, hard-boiled and halved
Candied ginger root, sliced

Preheat oven to 375°.

Melt the butter and blend in the flour. Add the milk, and heat, stirring constantly. Mix in the salt, pepper, and curry, and stir, cooking gently for a few minutes. Place the eggs in an ovenproof dish and carefully pour the sauce over them. Heat for 15 to 20 minutes, sprinkle with ginger root, and serve immediately.

Serves 6

Desserts

si fa lauoreri di latte

neuene si fa

Luochi freschi done fa lauoreri de latte

latte mele si fa

Peaches Miranda

PETER SPERLING
Public Education

Decorate with candied violets and black grapes and serve over vanilla ice cream, accompanied by tequila which has been kept in the freezer. The sauce should be syrupy from the grenadine, the peaches soft, and the whole an odd greenish color.

Lemon juice
6 *very* ripe peaches, peeled, halved, and pitted
  (or canned)
½ cup superfine sugar
1 small can guava nectar
A bit of orange juice
Grenadine
Tequila

Drip a trace of lemon juice over the peaches and cover with the sugar. Mix the guava nectar, orange juice, and grenadine, and pour over the peaches. Add as much tequila as you like, and refrigerate for at least an hour.

Serves 6

Cazzolo conil mamco   busiato

Pears in Grenadine

ELIZABETH E. GARDNER
European Paintings

For the sweet tooth.

2 halves canned Bartlett pears (regular or dietetic)
  per serving, drained
Grenadine
Vanilla ice cream

Cover the pears with grenadine and simmer until they have absorbed some of the syrup and are colored red. Serve hot or cold over ice cream.

Walter Hauser's "Coupe Alfonso XIII"

VERA K. OSTOIA
Medieval Art

Walter Hauser was Senior Research Fellow in the Department of Near Eastern Art and also Curator of the Library for many years.

> 1 can apricots
> Sugar
> 1 portion lemon sherbert per person
> Fresh raspberries

Simmer the apricots in a double boiler until they become a mush. Add sugar to taste, and cook for another 5 minutes. Put through a sieve (mixture should be quite thick). Cover the sherbert with raspberries, and top with the apricot syrup.

Seafoam Mousse

JOHN BUCHANAN
Director's Office

My wife's recipe, for a hot summer's day.

> 1 can (30 ounces) pears
> 1 package lime gelatin
> 1 package (8 ounces) cream cheese
> ¼ cup chopped walnuts
> 1 cup (½ pint) heavy cream
> Fresh raspberries, or 1 package frozen ones,
> drained

Drain the pears, reserving 1 cup of the juice. Heat the juice (do not boil), and add lime gelatin. Let mixture cool to room temperature. Combine the drained pears with the cream cheese and put through a food mill or potato masher. Add the nuts and pear juice-gelatin mixture. Combine well. Whip the cream and fold in. Pour into a serving bowl or ring mold, cover tightly, and refrigerate for 6 hours (it can be made several days in advance). Serve with the raspberries.

Serves 6

Tall Dessert

CARL C. DAUTERMAN
Western European Arts

May be varied in many ways: vanilla ice cream with ginger ale; chocolate ice cream with cream soda; coffee, mocha, or espresso ice cream with cream soda and Kahlúa or Tía María; vanilla ice cream with Cherry Heering; chocolate ice cream with crème de menthe.

> Milk
> Ice cream
> Flavored charged soda
> 1 teaspoon Drambuie
> Unsweetened whipped cream

Pour 1 inch of milk into a tall tumbler and add a generous portion of your favorite ice cream. Tilt the glass and pour in enough soda to almost fill the glass. Gently stir in the Drambuie. Float a generous dollop of whipped cream on top.

Mousse au Chocolat "Pas Cuite"

CATHERINE NEGROPONTE
Drawings

Serve this mousse with whipped cream and champagne.

> 1 package (8 ounces) sweet chocolate
> 1 tablespoon coffee or water
> 8 egg yolks
> 10 egg whites
> Grated chocolate

Melt the chocolate with coffee or water in a double boiler and cool slightly. Beat the egg yolks until pale and stir into chocolate (if it starts to harden, use an electric mixer). Beat the egg whites until stiff and fold into chocolate mixture. Pour into a serving bowl or individual dishes. Chill up to 24 hours. Sprinkle with grated chocolate.

Serves 6

Chocolate Mousse Flavored with Orange

LINDA SIPRESS
Bulletin and Calendar/News

Dorothy Bauman gave me this recipe when we worked together on the Museum's Centennial festivities.

4 eggs, separated
¼ cup sugar
1 package (6 ounces) chocolate bits
4 tablespoons strong coffee
½ pound butter, softened and cut into small pieces
¼ – ½ cup Grand Marnier
Pinch salt
Freshly grated orange peel
Chocolate sprinkles
Whipped cream (optional)

Beat egg yolks and sugar until mixture is thick and pale yellow. Cook over hot water until slightly thickened, stirring constantly. Melt the chocolate with the coffee over hot water. Remove from heat and beat in the pieces of butter one by one until you have a smooth cream. Combine chocolate with the egg yolks and add Grand Marnier to taste. Beat the egg whites until stiff, add the salt, and fold them into the chocolate mixture. Pour into pot de crème cups or a bowl and decorate with orange peel and chocolate sprinkles. Chill. Serve with whipped cream if you wish.

Serves 4

pignatta

Chocolate Icebox Cake

ANITA MULLER
Sales

A pretty party dessert.

3 packages (3 ounces each) ladyfingers,
  split lengthwise
2 packages Baker's German sweet chocolate
2½ tablespoons water or coffee
2 tablespoons granulated sugar
1 teaspoon vanilla
4 eggs (if very large, use 3)
1 cup (½ pint) heavy cream
A sprinkle of confectioner's sugar
1 drop almond extract

Line the sides and then the bottom of a springform pan with lady-fingers, filling in the gaps on the bottom with smaller pieces. Melt the chocolate in the top of a double boiler with the water or coffee, granulated sugar, and vanilla. As soon as it is smooth remove from heat and cool slightly. Mix in the eggs, one at a time. Beat until perfectly smooth. Spread evenly over the ladyfingers and cover with another layer of ladyfingers. Whip the cream, adding the confectioner's sugar and almond extract. Spread on top of the cake and refrigerate for several hours. Remove springform before serving.

  The ingredients as given above fill the ladyfinger mold about half-way to the top. For an even richer cake, double the amount of chocolate, the ingredients that are melted with it, and the eggs, making another layer before the final whipped cream.

Serves 6 to 8

Baked Fudge Dessert

PAGE AYRES
Drawings

Diabolically rich—halfway between a brownie and a pot de crème. Serve with whipped cream. From Dean Walker, a former graduate intern in the department.

2 cups sugar

½ cup flour

½ cup cocoa

4 eggs, well beaten

½ pound butter, melted

2 teaspoons vanilla

1 cup chopped pecans

Preheat oven to 300°.

Mix sugar, flour, and cocoa. Add to the beaten eggs and blend thoroughly. Add the butter, vanilla, and nuts. Pour into a pan or glass baking dish (9 by 9 inches) and place it in a pan of hot water. Bake for about 45 minutes. It may take a few minutes longer; you can tell by inserting a silver knife—it will have the consistency of custard but will not be stiff. As it cools it will become more firm. Cut in squares and serve.

    May be made a day ahead.

Serves 8 to 10

Calvados Soufflé

ASHTON HAWKINS
Secretary

Mr. Hawkins, a bachelor, impresses his guests with this spectacular dessert.

Butter

Granulated sugar

8 egg yolks

½ cup Calvados

10 egg whites

Pinch salt

Confectioner's sugar

Preheat oven to 425–450°.

Butter a 2-quart soufflé dish and sprinkle with granulated sugar, shaking out the excess. Tie a buttered wax paper collar around the dish, extending about 2 inches above edge. Beat the egg yolks in the top of a double boiler and slowly add 1 cup granulated sugar. Place over hot (not boiling) water, and continue to beat until it thickens. When the mixture coats the spoon remove from heat and stand the pot in ice water. Stir in the Calvados. Can be done in advance to this point.

When you are ready to cook the soufflé, beat the egg whites with a whisk in an unlined copper bowl. When soft peaks form, sprinkle on 1 tablespoon granulated sugar and beat like mad. When the egg whites form stiff peaks, fold them, a third at a time, into the egg yolk mixture. Fold quickly and lightly; don't worry if it looks a bit unmixed. Spoon into the soufflé dish and bake for 20 to 25 minutes, until the top is brownish. Sprinkle with confectioner's sugar, cut off the paper collar, and serve. The soufflé will be slightly unset in the middle, but the better for it.

Serves 8

Carol's Pie Dessert

JOHANNA HECHT
Western European Arts

From a one-time neighbor. It's very rich—like a giant brownie, crisp around the edges and fudge sauce in the middle. Serve with vanilla ice cream. I especially loved it when I was twelve. Forgive the Chinese restaurant–style instructions.

GROUP A	¾ cup sugar
	1 cup sifted flour
	2 teaspoons baking powder
	½ teaspoon salt
GROUP B	1 square bitter chocolate
	2 tablespoons butter
	½ cup milk
	1 teaspoon vanilla
GROUP C	½ cup brown sugar
	½ cup sugar
	4 tablespoons cocoa
	1 cup strong coffee

Preheat oven to 350°.

Mix and sift ingredients in Group A. Heat ingredients in Group B over hot water until butter and chocolate melt. Combine A and B and pour into a *well-greased* 10-inch pie plate. Combine ingredients in Group C and sprinkle over batter in pie plate. Pour coffee on top of everything. Bake 30 to 40 minutes; don't expect it to be done in the middle. Cool and serve.

Serves 6

Soufflé au Grand Marnier

BRUCE POPKIN
Sales

Classic and delicious.

> 2 tablespoons softened butter
> Granulated sugar
> 5 egg yolks
> ⅓ cup Grand Marnier (or other orange-flavored liqueur)
> 1 tablespoon grated orange rind
> 7 egg whites
> ¼ teaspoon cream of tartar (omit if using a copper bowl)
> Confectioner's sugar

Preheat oven to 425°.

Heavily butter a 6-cup soufflé dish. Pour 3 tablespoons granulated sugar into the dish, cover all the surfaces, and knock out the excess sugar. Beat the egg yolks with a whisk in an enamel saucepan and gradually add ⅓ cup granulated sugar, beating until the eggs fall back in a ribbon when the whisk is lifted. Set the pan into a larger pan of water that almost simmers. Stir with a rubber spatula or wooden spoon until the mixture feels warm to the touch; remove from heat. Add liqueur and orange rind. Transfer the mixture to a glass bowl and set it into a larger bowl filled with ice cubes. Stir until cool and leave on the ice. With a large whisk beat the egg whites until very stiff in an unlined copper bowl. If not available, use any material but aluminum and add cream of tartar. Mix a large

127

glob of the whites into the egg yolks, and then gently fold that mixture back into the egg whites. Carefully pour into the soufflé dish, filling to within 2 inches of the top. Smooth the top with a spatula. To form a cap insert the tip of the spatula in the mixture and draw a circle. Bake for a few minutes, reduce heat to 400°, and bake 25 minutes. Sprinkle with confectioner's sugar and serve immediately.

Serves 4

Plum Tart

ANITA MULLER
Sales

An unusual, shortbreadlike pastry. Serve with whipped cream. Peaches, strawberries, or apples may be substituted for the plums very successfully.

PASTRY 1 cup flour
½ cup ground almonds
¼ pound salted butter, at room temperature
1 package (3 ounces) cream cheese, at room temperature

FRUIT 1¼ pounds plums, washed, halved, and pitted
¾ cup sugar mixed with ¾ cup water
Pinch nutmeg

Preheat oven to 350°.

Pastry. Combine the flour and almonds, and cut in the butter and cream cheese. Shape into a ball and refrigerate for 30 minutes to 1 hour. Flatten the ball with the palm of your hand and pat it into a 9-inch pie plate, working it up the sides of the plate like a pie crust. The dough will be slightly crumbly and will have streaks of cream cheese. Bake until golden brown, about 30 minutes.

Fruit. Place the plums in a pan with the sugar water syrup. Cook, basting constantly. Add nutmeg. When the plums are soft but firm remove them from the syrup and cool. Continue to cook syrup until thick. Arrange plums on the pastry and dab with a little of the syrup.

Serves 6

Apple Sour Cream Pie

ROBIE ROGGE
Publications

This is the best thing I make; good warm or cold.

PIE 2 tablespoons flour

¾ cup sugar

¾ teaspoon cinnamon

⅛ teaspoon salt

1 egg

½ teaspoon vanilla

1 cup (½ pint) sour cream

6 medium apples, peeled, pared, and sliced

A 9-inch graham cracker crust

TOPPING ⅓ cup sugar

⅓ cup flour

¾ teaspoon cinnamon

¼ cup butter, creamed

Preheat oven to 400°.

Pie. Combine all pie ingredients except apples and crust. Add the apples and pour mixture into crust. Bake for 15 minutes, reduce heat to 350°, and bake 30 minutes.

Topping. Combine topping ingredients and crumble over pie. Bake at 400° for 10 minutes.

Serve warm or cold.

Pecan Pie Teréz

KNUD NIELSEN
Conservation

Conserua bassa

Good recipes for pecan pie are hard to find. I got this one from a neighbor.

> 3 eggs
> ½ teaspoon salt
> 1 cup sugar
> 1 cup light or dark corn syrup
> 1 teaspoon vanilla
> 1 tablespoon butter, melted
> 1 cup pecans
> 1 unbaked 10-inch pie shell

Preheat oven to 350°.

Beat eggs with the salt and sugar until smooth. Stir in the corn syrup, vanilla, butter, and pecans. Pour into the pie shell and bake for 30 minutes; reduce heat to 325° and bake 15 minutes longer. Serve warm or cold.

Date Pie

ELIZABETH R. USHER
Library

A delicious first cousin of pecan pie. Serve with whipped cream or ice cream.

> 2 eggs
> ¾ cup sugar
> ¼ cup melted butter
> 4 teaspoons milk
> ⅛ teaspoon salt
> ½ cup diced dates
> ½ cup chopped walnuts
> ½ teaspoon vanilla
> 1 unbaked pie shell

Preheat oven to 400°.

Mix by hand eggs, sugar, butter, milk, and salt. Add dates, nuts, and vanilla. Pour into pie shell and bake for 35 to 40 minutes.

Miss Adelaide Cahill's Pumpkin Pie with Molasses Meringue

VERA K. OSTOIA
Medieval Art

Miss Cahill was the Museum's archivist for many years. Her pie takes some doing, but is well worth it.

FILLING
- 1 cup light cream (or whole milk)
- ¾ cup sugar (brown or white)
- 1½ cups cooked pumpkin, strained
- 1 scant teaspoon salt
- ½ teaspoon ginger
- ½ teaspoon cinnamon
- ½ teaspoon cloves (optional)
- ¼ teaspoon vanilla
- 1 tablespoon molasses
- 1 egg
- 2 egg yolks (reserve whites for meringue)
- A 9-inch unbaked pastry shell

MERINGUE
- 2 tablespoons molasses
- 3 tablespoons sugar
- 2 egg whites (reserved from filling)
- ⅛ teaspoon cream of tartar
- Few grains salt
- ¼ cup chopped nuts (walnuts or pecans)

ſuſator ouato

Preheat oven to 450°.

Filling. Combine cream, sugar, and pumpkin, and mix well. Add the salt, spices, vanilla, and molasses, and mix thoroughly again. Beat the egg and egg yolks, and add them to the pumpkin mixture.

Pour into pie shell and bake for 20 minutes; reduce heat to 325° and bake for 45 minutes longer, until the filling is *firm*. Cool slightly.

Meringue. Cook the molasses with 2 tablespoons of the sugar until it reaches 238° on a candy thermometer. Cool slightly. Beat the egg whites until frothy and add cream of tartar and salt. Continue beating until peaks form. Add the remaining tablespoon of sugar. Pour the molasses into the egg whites *very* slowly, in a *very* thin thread. Now hurry. Spread the meringue over the pumpkin filling so that it overlaps onto the crust a bit. Sprinkle with the nuts, and bake at 325° for 15 to 20 minutes. Watch the pie *carefully*, for the meringue scorches easily.

Frozen Lemon Pie

JOHANNA HECHT
Western European Arts

There are a lot of recipes sort of like this one, but most are fluffy—not as dense or rich. A wonderful summer dessert.

15 vanilla wafers, crushed

3 eggs, separated

½ cup sugar

⅛ teaspoon salt

¼ cup lemon juice

1 tablespoon grated lemon rind

1 cup (½ pint) heavy cream (at least a day old is best for whipping)

Line a 10-inch pie plate with half the crushed wafers, spreading evenly over the bottom and sides, and reserve the rest. Beat the egg yolks with the sugar, salt, and lemon juice in the top of a double boiler. Stir constantly over hot water (being careful not to let the eggs curdle) until the mixture thickens and coats a metal spoon—this should take about 15 minutes. Add lemon rind and cool. Beat the cream and egg whites separately until each is stiff. Fold the cream and then the whites into the cooled yolk mixture and turn into the pie plate. Sprinkle with the reserved wafer crumbs. Freeze until firm. Remove from refrigerator exactly 30 minutes before serving. Leftovers may be refrozen.

Tarte Hollandaise

CHARLES WRIGHTSMAN
Trustee

We were so delighted to receive the Wrightsmans' recipe in French that we include it just as their chef wrote it. A translation, which we hope does it justice, follows.

Étendre une abaisse de feuilletage de 2 lignes d'èpaisseur, sur une plaque légèrement beurrée. Imprimer légèrement dans l'abaisse un cercle qui défiinira la grandeur de la tarte. Garnir le centre de crême d'amandes "en garder 2 cuilléres à soupe en resèrve." Mouiller le tour à l'aide d'un pinceau humecter d'eau. Poser une autre abaisse de feuilletage sur la première de façon quelle recouvre la marque laissée par le cercle. Poser le cercle sur le dessus de la tarte de façon qu'il se trouve superpose à la marque laisser sur la première abaisse. Découper à l'aide d'un couteau et aplatir les bords avec la paume de la main. Napper le dessus de la tarte avec le reste de crême d'amandes et soupoudrer de sucre glace "powder sugar." Tracer légèrement les parts à l'aide d'un couteau. Cuire à feu doux 45 minutes pour une tarte de 5 personnes.

Crême d'amandes. Une once et demi de beurre en crême dans une terrine ou un bol. Sur un papier mélanger 4 onces et demi de poudre d'amandes blanche avec 6 onces et demi de sucre fin. Additioner ce mélange au beurre et ajouter 2 oeufs. Travailler à l'aide d'une cuillere vigoureusement.

mortar

> 1½ tablespoons butter
> 4½ ounces powdered white almonds
> Confectioner's sugar
> 2 eggs
> Puff pastry dough

Preheat oven to 350°.

To make almond paste, place butter in a bowl. Combine the almonds and 1½ cups confectioner's sugar, and mix them with the butter. Add the eggs and cream vigorously with a spoon.

Spread a layer of puff paste dough of double thickness on a lightly buttered cookie sheet. Draw a circle in the dough the desired size of the tart. Spread the almond cream in the center, reserving 2 tablespoons. Moisten the edges of the circle with a wet pastry brush.

133

buriglia

Place a second layer of pastry over the first, making sure that it is large enough to cover the original circle. Retrace the circle onto the second layer. Trim the excess pastry with a knife and press the edges of the two layers together with the palm of the hand. Spread the remaining almond cream over the top of the tart and sprinkle with confectioner's sugar. Five portions may be lightly etched with a knife at this point. Bake for 45 minutes.

Serves 5

Bavarian Cheese Cake with Graham Nut Crust

JOHN BUCHANAN
Director's Office

The almond extract gives my wife's cake a unique flavor.

CRUST
- 1¾ cups fine graham cracker crumbs
- ¼ cup finely chopped walnuts
- ½ teaspoon cinnamon
- ½ cup butter or margarine, melted

FILLING
- 2 eggs, well beaten
- 2 packages (8 ounces each) cream cheese, softened
- 1 cup sugar
- ¼ teaspoon salt
- 2 teaspoons vanilla
- ½ teaspoon almond extract
- 2 cups (1 pint) sour cream

Preheat oven to 375°.

Crust. Mix all crust ingredients well. Reserving 3 tablespoons of the mixture, press the remainder into the bottom and 2½ inches up the sides of a 9-inch springform pan or pie plate.

Filling. Combine the eggs, cream cheese, sugar, salt, vanilla, and almond extract and beat until smooth. Blend in the sour cream, and pour mixture into the crust. Sprinkle with reserved crust mixture, and bake for 35 minutes, or until set. Cool and chill well, about 4 to 5 hours.

Serves 10 (approximately)

Cheese Cake

ELIZABETH R. USHER
Library

Takes work, but the cheese cake is excellent.

CRUST   3 cups crushed graham crackers
         ¼ pound butter, melted
         ¼ cup sugar

FILLING 2 packages (8 ounces each) cream cheese
         3 eggs
         ½ cup sugar (more or less, to taste)
         1 teaspoon vanilla

TOPPING 2 cups (1 pint) sour cream
         ¼ cup sugar (more or less, to taste)
         1 teaspoon vanilla
         Cinnamon or nutmeg

Preheat oven to 375°.

Crust. Line springform pan with two pieces of aluminum foil, one on bottom, one on sides (if you do not have a springform pan, an unlined Pyrex one will do). Mix crust ingredients well and press them into pan, saving some for the topping.

Filling. Beat the filling ingredients well with an electric mixer on high speed or by hand. Pour into crust and bake for 20 minutes. Cool for 45 minutes.

Topping. Preheat oven to 475°. Beat together sour cream, sugar, and vanilla. Spread lightly on cooled cake. Cover with reserved graham cracker crumbs and sprinkle with cinnamon or nutmeg. Bake for 10 minutes. Refrigerate for at least 24 hours, so that crust and custard are well set.

Serves 10

navicella alta

MMA Cheese Cake

CHEF MARIO
Restaurant

Will keep fresh in the refrigerator for up to three weeks.

4 packages (8 ounces each) cream cheese, at room
   temperature
1 cup sugar
3 eggs
Juice and grated rind of ½ lemon
1 teaspoon vanilla
Butter
¼ cup corn flakes, crushed to a powder

Preheat oven to 325°.

Mix thoroughly all ingredients except the butter and corn flakes.
Heavily butter an 8-inch cake pan, and coat it completely with the
crushed corn flakes. Pour in the cheese mixture and place in a metal
dish containing about ⅓ inch water. Bake for 1½ hours. Turn off
the oven and let the cake stand in it for an additional 30 minutes.
Remove from oven and cool for 45 minutes before taking from pan.

Serves 12

Adirondack Griddle Cakes

JOHN WALSH, JR.
European Paintings

These are a sort of backwoods crêpe that have been a special dessert
since the early days of Adirondack resort hotels. Each serving con-
sists of three 6- to 7-inch griddle cakes, with hot maple sauce in
between and on top, and crowned with a glob of whipped cream.
It is least hectic to make the whipped cream first, then the griddle
batter, then the maple sauce, then the griddle cakes.

1½ cups pancake mix (or 1½ cups flour mixed with
   ¼ teaspoon salt and 2 teaspoons baking powder)
1½ cups milk (more if needed)
2 beaten eggs

1½ tablespoons vegetable oil
8 ounces pure maple syrup
½ cup heavy cream

Griddle cakes. Combine pancake mix, milk, eggs, and oil, and stir until the batter is only somewhat lumpy (it should be a fairly thin, eggy batter; if the first griddle cakes are thick, add milk to it). Grease a skillet or griddle lightly and place over a medium heat until a drop of water bounces a bit before evaporating. Pour 6- to 7-inch puddles of batter, swirling gently to spread them thinner. Turn the griddle cakes when bubbles cover the surface and the edges are light brown. As they are done, remove to a warm oven. Makes approximately 12 griddle cakes.

Maple sauce. Heat the maple syrup and allow to boil for 3 or 4 minutes, no longer. Put the hot syrup in a blender and beat until frothy, about 5 minutes. The sauce can be kept warm for half an hour or so without losing its consistency.

Whipped cream. In a thoroughly chilled mixing bowl beat the cream until it forms soft peaks. Keep in the refrigerator until ready to use.

Serves 4

Rice Pudding

MARGARET HARTT
Public Education

People can't believe that such a small amount of rice can produce a creamy pudding, but it does.

2 heaping tablespoons rice
1 quart milk
¼ cup sugar
Optional: raisins, grated lemon rind, vanilla
Nutmeg

Preheat oven to 300°.

Mix the ingredients in a baking dish and place in oven. After the first half hour stir every 15 minutes, removing the film should one form and puff up. The pudding should bubble very gently; if it appears to be cooking too fast, lower the heat. Cook for 2 to 2½ hours, or until it becomes creamy. Do not allow the pudding to become dense, for it will thicken after the cooking. Remove from oven and stir occasionally as it cools. Sprinkle with nutmeg and refrigerate.

Serves 4

Philadelphia Vanilla

WESTON NAEF
Prints and Photographs

When ice cream was first introduced in France in the 1840s it was said that the treat was so good that to eat it must be a sin. The sinful delicacy was very likely not far removed in taste from what we call "Philadelphia Vanilla," which could not be made from more venal ingredients.

> 1 quart heavy cream
> ¾ cup sugar
> 3-inch vanilla bean (or 1½ teaspoons vanilla
>   extract)
> A few grains salt

The day before the ice cream is to be frozen, warm the cream (do not boil). Stir in the sugar until dissolved, scrape in the contents of the vanilla bean (or add extract), and add the salt. Refrigerate mixture. The next day freeze the custard by hand ice cream maker or with an electric machine.

This is a basic recipe, easily adaptable to other flavors. Chocolate and other flavors derived from syrups may be made by substituting light cream for the heavy cream. Fresh fruit, crushed or sliced, should be added just before churning.

1 quart

Cookies, Cakes, & Breads

Almond Icebox Cookies

ELIZABETH R. USHER
Library

Very crisp.

> 1 pound butter
> 2 cups sugar
> 4 large eggs
> 1 teaspoon vanilla
> 1 pound blanched almonds, chopped
> 5 cups flour

Preheat oven to 350°.

Cream butter, add sugar gradually, and mix in rest of ingredients. Form dough into rolls that are about 2 inches in diameter and refrigerate overnight (or longer). Slice *as thinly as possible* and bake until light brown (about 8 minutes).

About 30 cookies

Raisin Sugar Cookies

J. RICHARDSON DILWORTH
Trustee

This and the following are my wife's classic recipes for these delicious old-fashioned cookies.

Coltelli da torta

> ½ pound butter
> 1 tablespoon maple syrup
> 1 cup sugar
> 3 cups flour
> 1 teaspoon baking soda
> Raisins

Preheat oven to 350°.

Beat butter, syrup, and sugar into a cream. Mix in flour and baking soda. Roll thinly and cut with cookie cutter. Place a raisin in the middle of each and bake on a greased cookie sheet until light brown.

About 20 cookies

Sand Tarts

J. RICHARDSON DILWORTH
Trustee

forcina

2 ¼ cups sugar

2 cups butter

2 eggs, well beaten

4 cups flour

2 cups chopped walnuts

2 egg whites, beaten with a little water

Cinnamon combined with sugar

Chopped walnuts

Preheat oven to 350°.

Combine sugar, butter, eggs, flour, and chopped nuts. Refrigerate until cold. Roll thin. Cut with cookie cutter, place on greased cookie sheet, and brush with egg white mixture. Dust with cinnamon sugar and sprinkle with a few chopped nuts. Bake for about 10 minutes.

About 40 cookies

Scotch Shortbread

J. RICHARDSON DILWORTH
Trustee

So much better than the kind that comes in a tin.

½ pound butter

½ cup sugar

Pinch salt

2 cups flour

Granulated sugar

Preheat oven to 450°.

Cream butter, sugar, and salt, and work in flour. Press dough into an 8-by-8-inch tin pan (ungreased), about ¼ inch thick. Prick top with fork. Bake for 10 minutes at 450°, then lower heat to 350° and continue cooking until golden brown on top. Sprinkle with granulated sugar and cut into squares as wished while still warm. Let cool in pan.

English Tea Cakes

MARISE JOHNSON
Far Eastern Art

From my grandmother.

ferro da maccerom

Scringhe

1½ cups flour

½ cup sugar

¼ teaspoon salt

2 teaspoons baking powder

2 tablespoons honey

¼ pound butter

½ cup currants

1 egg, beaten

2 tablespoons milk

Few drops vanilla

Preheat oven to 450°.

Mix the dry ingredients and then add the rest. Place in teaspoon-size balls on a greased cookie sheet. Bake for 20 minutes, until golden brown.

About 30 cookies

Lebkuchen

PETER FISCHER
Carpenter's Shop

My own recipe for these holiday cookies. May be decorated with almonds or fruits before baking; or frost with sugar mixed with a little liqueur or lemon juice. Also good coated with melted chocolate bits.

2 eggs

¾ cup granulated sugar, or 1 cup brown sugar

¾ cup ground or chopped mixed candied fruits

1 cup chopped almonds

1 teaspoon freshly grated lemon rind

4 tablespoons butter

½ cup honey

3 cups flour

¾ teaspoon baking powder

¾ teaspoon baking soda

1 teaspoon cinnamon

½ teaspoon cloves

½ teaspoon allspice

½ teaspoon mace

¼ teaspoon cardamom powder

¼ teaspoon anise

Preheat oven to 350°.

Beat the eggs with the sugar, and add fruit, almonds, and lemon rind. In a small pan heat the butter, honey, and ¼ cup water. Add to the egg mixture. Sift together all the remaining ingredients and mix well with egg mixture (the dough may be stored in the refrigerator for 1 or 2 days). Shape cookies with a large cutter or drop from a spoon. Bake on a well-buttered cookie sheet for approximately 20 minutes.

Refrigerate, individually wrapped, in a tightly covered container. Will keep for 6 months (if nobody finds them).

About 30 cookies

Sperone da pasticiero

Kourabiedes

CYNTHIA LAMBROS
Drawings

The secret to these glorious cookies is inundating them with powdered sugar while they are still warm. The recipe is from my mother-in-law, Mrs. John Lambros, of Farrell, Pennsylvania.

1 pound sweet butter

Confectioner's sugar

2 egg yolks

½ cup orange juice

¼ cup ouzo, cognac, or whiskey

2 cups ground almonds (other nuts may be used,
   but almonds give the most authentic flavor)

5–5 ½ cups flour, sifted

Preheat oven to 350°.

Clarify the butter by heating it very slowly in a small pan (do not boil). Remove the scum from the top and cool. Slowly pour into a large mixing bowl, being very careful not to include any of the milky substance at the bottom. Refrigerate the clarified butter until very cold.

Add 2 tablespoons confectioner's sugar to the cold butter and beat it with an electric mixer. It should have the consistency of whipped cream. Beat the egg yolks in one at a time. Slowly add the orange juice and ouzo (or cognac or whiskey). Remove the bowl from the mixer. Mix in the nuts with a spatula, and then add the flour one cup at a time. Use your hand when the dough becomes heavy. Knead the dough for 10 minutes; it will be slightly crumbly at first, but will form a ball as you work it. Shape the cookies into the desired form (usually crescent-shaped) and place on an ungreased cookie sheet. Bake 20 to 25 minutes, or until light brown. Do not be discouraged at this point, for they look rather dry and unappealing. When they are cool enough to handle, roll each one in confectioner's sugar and then liberally sift more sugar over them.

The cookies will stay fresh for up to 3 weeks, nestled in powdered sugar in a tightly covered container.

About 60 cookies

Conserua grande

Maine Island Applesauce Cake

MORRISON HECKSCHER
American Wing

Elizabeth Prior of Louds Island, Maine, gave me this recipe for applesauce cake. She bakes the finest pies and cakes I know. The recipe seems to have originated on the island of Criehaven in the mid-nineteenth century; Elizabeth learned it from her grandmother. The island people used chicken grease instead of the shortening available today. Elizabeth improved upon the traditional version by adding the nuts, dates, raisins, and cherries. And it was at my request that she put this favorite recipe, heretofore handed down solely by oral tradition, into writing.

1 teaspoon baking soda
1 cup applesauce
½ cup cooking oil
1 cup sugar
1¾ cups flour
½ teaspoon salt
1 teaspoon cinnamon
½ teaspoon nutmeg
¼ teaspoon powdered cloves
1 cup raisins, ground (use a meat grinder)
¼ cup chopped nuts
1 small bottle maraschino cherries, chopped

Preheat oven to 350°.

Stir the baking soda into the applesauce and add oil and sugar. Mix in the flour, salt, and spices. Lastly, add the raisins, nuts, and cherries. Bake in a square pan for 1 hour (or more, if necessary).

tortera con il coperto

Big Cake
(mocha nut)

JOHANNA HECHT
Western European Arts

A terrific party cake, quite light and therefore good after a soggy meal. Because of the whipped cream in the frosting, it should be frozen until just before serving if done in advance.

CAKE
2 ¼ cups sifted cake flour
3 teaspoons baking powder
1 teaspoon salt
¾ cup granulated sugar
¾ cup brown sugar
8 eggs, separated
½ cup vegetable oil
2 teaspoons maple flavoring
½ teaspoon cream of tartar
1 cup chopped walnuts

[handwritten: ¾ c cold water]

FROSTING
½ cup cocoa
Granulated sugar
¼ cup milk
½ cup strong coffee
1 pint heavy cream

Preheat oven to 300°.

Cake. Sift together the flour, baking powder, salt, and white sugar; add the brown sugar. Make a well in these dry ingredients, and add the egg yolks, ¾ cup cold water, oil, and maple flavoring. Mix well. Beat the egg whites with the cream of tartar until stiff, but not dry. Gently fold the whites and walnuts into the batter. Turn into an ungreased angel food cake pan and bake at 300° for 40 minutes; raise heat to 350° and bake for another 50 minutes. *[handwritten: (1 hr & 20 min) 325° 40 min]*

Frosting. Combine cocoa and ½ cup granulated sugar, add milk, and mix. Gradually add the coffee, bring to a boil, and cook until a drop hardens in cold water, about 10 minutes. Cool well. When close to serving time, whip cream with 2 tablespoons of sugar and beat into cocoa mixture. Frost cake whole, or if a richer cake is wanted, split it in half horizontally and spread a layer of frosting (there is ample frosting for this).

fufatoro largo

146

Marble Cake

JEAN COHEN
Accounts Payable

Serve with fruit or for tea.

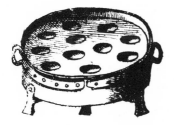

¾ cup butter

1½ cups sugar

4 eggs, separated

1 teaspoon baking powder

½ cup milk

2 cups cake flour

1 teaspoon vanilla

6 ounces German sweet chocolate, melted

Preheat oven to 350°.

Cream butter and add egg yolks. Combine baking powder with milk and add to butter and egg yolks alternately with flour. Mix well and add vanilla. Beat egg whites until stiff, and fold into batter. Pour all but a third of the batter in a buttered springform pan. Combine the remaining batter with the chocolate and fold gently into batter in pan so that ribbons of chocolate are visible. Bake 55 minutes.

Bundt Cake

BETT HOLENDER
Sculpture Reproduction Workshop

The chocolate chips do not melt completely in the baking, so the cake is punctuated with surprise nuggets.

1 package Duncan Hines Deep Chocolate cake mix

1 small package instant chocolate pudding

½ cup vegetable oil

½ cup warm water

1 cup (½ pint) sour cream

4 eggs

1 package (12 ounces) chocolate chips

Confectioner's sugar

Preheat oven to 350°.

Mix all ingredients except eggs, chocolate, and sugar. Add eggs one at a time. Beat well. Fold in the chocolate chips. Grease a bundt pan lightly and pour in mixture. Bake for 1 hour. Cool for 45 minutes and unmold. Sift confectioner's sugar over top. Do not refrigerate.

Meringue Cake

CECILE S. HERLIHY
Membership

Setacci doppio p speciarie et zucharo

Makes an unusual birthday cake—very light. Decorate with additional whipped cream and strawberries, if you wish.

CAKE	½ cup butter
	½ cup sugar
	4 egg yolks
	¼ cup milk
	½ teaspoon vanilla
	1 cup flour, sifted
	1¼ teaspoons baking powder
	½ teaspoon salt
MERINGUE	4 egg whites
	Pinch salt
	1 cup sugar
	1 teaspoon vanilla
	Walnuts or pecans, chopped
FILLING	1 cup heavy cream
	Fresh strawberries or raspberries (or frozen, thawed)

Preheat oven to 350°.

Cake. Cream the butter well with the sugar, and add the egg yolks one at a time. Add the remaining cake ingredients and beat vigorously for 2 minutes. Pour equal amounts of the batter into two 9-inch cake pans.

Meringue. Beat the egg whites with a pinch of salt. Gradually add the sugar and vanilla. Spread the meringue in uneven peaks over the batter in each pan, making sure that it touches the edges of the pans. Sprinkle the nuts on top of the meringue and bake for 35 minutes. Cool on a rack.

Assembling the cake. Whip the cream. If using frozen berries, drain them very thoroughly. Mix the berries into the whipped cream. Spread one-half of this filling over one layer of cake. Place the second layer on top, and coat with the remaining whipped cream. Refrigerate.

Serve very cold.

Serves 12

Count Nádasdy's Chocolate Cake

ELLEN ECKHARDT
Sales

A Hungarian recipe—very rich.

6 eggs, separated
½ pound sweet butter
1 heaping cup granulated sugar
¾ cup ground almonds
9 ounces Baker's sweet chocolate
½ cup (scant) flour, sifted
Granulated sugar

Preheat oven to 375°.

Mix the egg yolks with the butter until smooth. Add the granulated sugar, mix well, and add the almonds. Melt the chocolate in the top of a double boiler and add. Stir in the flour and mix until smooth. Beat the egg whites until stiff and fold into mixture. Pour into a buttered and floured 9-inch cake pan. Bake for about ¾ hour—it is done when the top is cooked, but the inside is still creamy (test often with a small knife). The cake wants close watching.

When the cake is still fairly hot, sprinkle it with granulated sugar. Heat a metal spatula with a wooden handle and press it down onto the sugar. Repeat, reheating the spatula, until most of the sugar is browned.

Bake the cake the day you serve it.

Sauerkraut Surprise Cake

RAY KRAFT
Service and Supply

One would never guess the surprise ingredient in this moist chocolate cake.

CAKE
- ¼ pound butter or margarine
- 1½ cups sugar
- 3 eggs
- 1 teaspoon vanilla
- 2 cups flour
- 1 teaspoon baking powder
- 1 teaspoon baking soda
- ¼ teaspoon salt
- 1 cup cocoa powder
- 1 bag or can (8 ounces) sauerkraut, well washed, drained, and chopped

FROSTING
- 1 package (6 ounces) semisweet chocolate bits
- 4 tablespoons butter or margarine
- ½ cup sour cream
- 1 teaspoon vanilla
- ¼ teaspoon salt
- 2½–2¾ cups confectioner's sugar, sifted

Preheat oven to 350°.

Cake. In a large bowl cream the butter or margarine and sugar until light. Beat in the eggs one at a time; add vanilla. Sift together the dry cake ingredients and beat slowly into the creamed mixture, alternating with 1 cup of water. Stir in the sauerkraut and turn into a greased and floured pan (13 by 9 by 12 inches). Bake for 35 to 40 minutes and cool in pan.

Frosting. Melt the chocolate with the butter or margarine over a low heat. Remove from heat and add sour cream, vanilla, and salt. Gradually add confectioner's sugar, beating until frosting reaches a spreading consistency.

Christmas Black Bun

JESSIE MCNAB DENNIS
Western European Arts

"Bun" is the old Scottish name for plum cake. It should be made several months, even a year, ahead of time and kept tightly covered in a cool place. A very rich cake—serve small, thin slices.

FILLING
2 pounds currants, washed and dried
2 pounds raisins, crushed
1 pound blanched almonds, chopped
½ pound mixed candied peel, chopped
4 cups flour
½ ounce ground cloves or cinnamon
½ ounce ground ginger
1 teaspoon Jamaica pepper
½ cup brown sugar
1 scant teaspoon baking soda
Buttermilk or beaten egg
1 tablespoon brandy

CRUST
4 cups flour
½ pound butter, softened
1 egg, beaten

Preheat oven to 350°

Filling. Mix the currants, raisins, almonds, and peel. In another bowl sift the flour with the cloves or cinnamon, ginger, and pepper. Add the sugar and baking soda, then the fruit mixture. Moisten with buttermilk or egg, and add the brandy.

Crust. Mix the flour and butter with enough water to make a stiff paste. Roll out thinly, and line a greased cake pan, reserving enough for the top. Press in the filling and cover with the remaining pastry. Make all secure and neat. With a long skewer make holes right down to the bottom of the cake. Prick all over the top with a fork, brush with beaten egg, and bake for about 4 hours.

Whole Wheat Bread with Poppy Seeds

HUGH R. CLOPTON
Superintendent's Office

When you bake this bread place a pan of water in the bottom of the oven—it keeps the bread from drying out and helps to make a thin, beautiful crust.

> 1 package yeast
> 1 egg
> 1 cup whole wheat flour, sifted
> 2 cups all-purpose flour, sifted
> ½ teaspoon salt
> 1 tablespoon sugar
> ½ cup milk
> 3 tablespoons butter, softened
> Poppy seeds

Preheat oven to 400°.

Dissolve the yeast in ½ cup warm water and mix in the egg. Allow mixture to come to room temperature. In a large bowl mix the dry ingredients, making a pocket in the middle. Pour in the yeast mixture and add the milk and butter. Knead for 10 minutes. Place in a warm place, covered with a damp towel, and allow to rise until double in size, 1 to 2 hours. Pound down and form into two long narrow loaves (French bread style). Allow to rise 1 more hour. Cut diagonal slashes in the dough and sprinkle with poppy seeds. Bake for 10 minutes at 400°, reduce heat to 325°, and bake for 40 minutes.

Coltelli mastri da battere

White or Whole Wheat Bread

RUTH GOTTLIEB
American Wing

Vary this bread by baking it in clay flower pots, for they act like a brick oven. Or make braids from the dough and brush them with egg yolk before baking.

raschiatore da banoho

Armiola da raschiare

WHITE	¾ ounces fresh yeast or 1 package dry yeast
	6 cups unbleached white flour
	1 teaspoon sugar
	1¼ cups milk
	3–4 tablespoons shortening or oil
	¼ cup sugar
	1 tablespoon salt
	2 eggs, slightly beaten
	Vegetable oil or water

WHOLE WHEAT	¾ ounce fresh yeast or 1 package dry yeast
	4 cups whole wheat flour
	2 cups unbleached white flour
	1 teaspoon sugar
	1¾ cups milk
	¼ cup molasses
	1 tablespoon salt
	3–4 tablespoons shortening or oil
	Vegetable oil or water

Mix the yeast with ¼ cup warm water. Place the flour in a very large bowl. Make a fist-sized hole in the center of the flour and pour yeast mixture into it. Work in a little of the surrounding flour to make a small ball. This is a trial dough, to test if your yeast is active. Sprinkle the dough with a little sugar. Cover the bowl with a damp cloth, put in a warm place (if necessary, a pan of warm water will do), and let the dough rise until almost double in size, about 30 minutes. If it rises, mix in the rest of the ingredients (except the oil or water used to brush on top of the dough before baking) and knead on a wood or enamel surface until smooth and elastic, about 10 minutes. Return to the bowl, cover with the damp cloth, and let rise until double in size, about 1 hour. Knead 5 minutes more. Divide in half and place in two greased and floured loaf pans. Let rise again until double in size, about 1 hour. Brush with oil for a soft crust, water for a hard one. Bake for about 45 minutes at 360° to 370°.

If you use flower pots, prepare by greasing them with shortening and baking empty in a 375° oven for ½ hour. Repeat twice more. They can then be used repeatedly.

Moist Gingerbread

LAURA MCLEOD
Funds Accounting

From the *MacLeod Family Cookbook*, 1966, a collection of clan recipes.

½ pound treacle
¼ pound butter or margarine
1 cup brown sugar
2 cups flour
⅔ cup ground rice
2 teaspoons cinnamon
2 teaspoons ginger
2 teaspoons allspice
1 teaspoon baking soda
2 eggs, separated
1 bottle lager beer

Preheat oven to 250°.

Melt the treacle, margarine, and sugar. Cool, then mix in dry ingredients, egg yolks, and beer. Beat the egg whites until stiff, and fold in. Pour into a greased pan and bake for 3 to 4 hours, until it starts to come away from the sides of the pan.

Iowa Gingerbread

MARISE JOHNSON
Far Eastern Art

A recipe from my Iowa ancestors.

2 teaspoons baking soda
1 cup hot coffee
½ cup softened butter
1 cup molasses
1 teaspoon ginger
1 teaspoon cinnamon
1 teaspoon cloves
2½ cups flour
1 cup raisins
2 eggs, well beaten

Preheat oven to 375°.

In a bowl dissolve baking soda in coffee. Add rest of ingredients and pour into a lightly greased baking pan (12 by 9 by 2 inches). Bake for 30 to 40 minutes, until a fork inserted into middle comes out clean.

Banana Bread

AMY BLUMENTHAL
Membership

Good any time, but really special toasted for breakfast.

3 ripe or overripe bananas
1 cup sugar
1 egg
1½ cups flour
4 tablespoons butter, melted
1 teaspoon baking soda
1 teaspoon salt

Preheat oven to 325°.

Peel and mash bananas, and stir in remaining ingredients. Pour into Teflon or buttered loaf pan (8½ by 4½ by 2½ inches). Bake 1 hour.

155

Bishop's Bread

LEONE C. MCKEEVER
Infirmary

A coffee cake with a cinnamon flavor.

> 2 cups brown sugar
>
> 2 ½ cups flour
>
> ½ cup shortening
>
> 1 teaspoon cinnamon
>
> 3 teaspoons baking powder
>
> 1 egg, beaten
>
> ¾ cup milk
>
> ½ teaspoon salt

Preheat oven to 400°.

Cream together sugar, flour, and shortening. Save ¾ cup of this mixture for the top of the bread. To the remainder add the rest of the ingredients in the order given. Place in a lightly greased shallow pan. Cover with the reserved mixture. Bake for 45 minutes to 1 hour.

Date and Nut Bread

CONNIE ASHLEY
Sales

A never-fail recipe for this versatile bread.

> 1 cup raisins
>
> 1 cup chopped dates
>
> 1 cup chopped walnuts
>
> 1 heaping teaspoon baking soda
>
> 2 eggs
>
> 1 cup sugar
>
> 2 cups flour
>
> 1 teaspoon vanilla

Place raisins, dates, and nuts in a bowl. Add baking soda and 1 cup of boiling water, and cool. In another bowl beat eggs and sugar; add flour and vanilla. Combine the mixtures. Pour into a greased 8-inch loaf pan, set oven at 325°, and bake for 1 ½ hours.

Scones from Scotland

LAURA MCLEOD
Funds Accounting

From the *MacLeod Family Cookbook*, 1966, a collection of clan recipes. This one was contributed by Alice MacNab of MacNab Killin, Perthshire. Serve the scones warm with butter and jam.

4 tablespoons butter or margarine
2½ cups flour
1 heaping tablespoon baking powder
Pinch of salt
¾–1 cup milk

Preheat oven to 450°.

Cut the butter or margarine into the flour and add baking powder and salt. Slowly mix in the milk until the mixture forms a dough. Divide into about 12 heaps and place on a floured cookie sheet. Bake for about 12 minutes, until slightly browned.

About 12 scones

Yorkshire Pudding

CHRISTINE ROUSSEL
Sculpture Reproduction Workshop

A popoverlike Yorkshire pudding that is a great addition to Sunday lunch.

⅞ cup flour
½ teaspoon salt
½ cup milk
2 eggs, beaten
Drippings from roast beef

Preheat oven to 400°.

In a bowl sift together flour and salt. Pour the milk into the center of the flour mixture. Add ½ cup water to the eggs and beat into the flour and milk until large bubbles appear on the surface. Grease a skillet or heavy iron pan with the drippings from the roast and heat it. Pour batter into the hot pan. Bake 20 minutes at 400°, lower heat to 350°, and bake 10 minutes more. Serve immediately, with roast beef, of course.

Serves 4

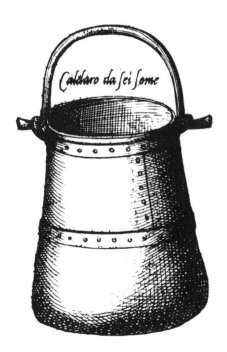

Caldaro da sei some

Menus & Miscellaneous

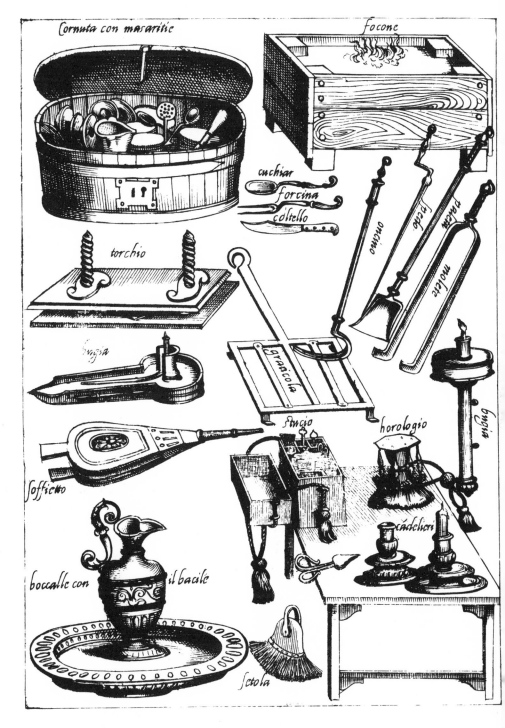

Choong-Heup's Feast

ANITA KOH
Ancient Near Eastern Art

When my husband's brother, who is a marvelous Korean cook, visited us, he taught me several dishes. This is the first meal he made for us, served with a hearty soup (page 32), kimchi (page 165), rice (page 104), and a little warm sake.

MENU   CUCUMBER SALAD
BEAN SPROUTS
POTATOES KAMCHA NAMUL
FRIED BEAN CURD

CUCUMBER SALAD
1 cucumber, washed but not peeled
Salt
1 tablespoon sesame oil
1 teaspoon toasted sesame seeds
Pinch red pepper flakes
½ teaspoon sugar

Cut cucumber in paper-thin slices, salt lightly, and let sit 10 to 15 minutes. Squeeze dry with paper towels. In a small mixing bowl combine remaining ingredients. Mix with cucumber and chill.

BEAN SPROUTS
½ pound soybean or mung bean sprouts
Chicken broth or water
1 tablespoon red pepper flakes
1–2 tablespoons sesame oil
1–2 tablespoons toasted sesame seeds
1 tablespoon soy sauce

Cook the bean sprouts in broth or water for about 10 minutes, until tender. Rinse to cool, and drain. Add the remaining ingredients, mix, and chill.

POTATOES	2 tablespoons sesame oil or butter
KAMCHA	1 large onion, sliced
NAMUL	2 potatoes, peeled and sliced into strips ½ inch
	wide, ⅛ inch thick, 1–2 inches long
	1 tablespoon toasted sesame seeds
	3–4 tablespoons soy sauce
	1 large clove garlic, crushed
	2 dried mushrooms, soaked and sliced (optional)

Heat the sesame oil or butter in a heavy skillet, add the onions and potatoes, and cook over a high heat for 2 to 3 minutes. Add the remaining ingredients and cook until the potatoes are tender. Keep warm until ready to serve.

FRIED	1 bean curd, drained, dried, and sliced into pieces
BEAN	1½ by 1 by ¼ inches
CURD	Soy sauce
	Sesame oil
	Toasted sesame seeds
	Red pepper powder (optional)

Marinate the pieces of bean curd in soy sauce for 10 minutes, then drain. Fry bean curd in a skillet with a little sesame oil for about 5 minutes. Sprinkle with sesame seeds, a dash of sesame oil, and red pepper powder if you wish.

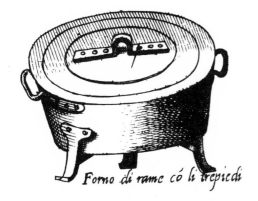

Forno di rame có li trepiedi

Sunday Night Menu

JAMES J. RORIMER
(1905–1966)

Mr. Rorimer, late Director of the Museum, took great pleasure in cooking for colleagues. Mrs. Rorimer writes, "We used to spend our Sundays preparing this meal, always with a gang hoping to have their Museum problems solved before Monday morning."

MENU   CLAM BROTH
SUNDAY NIGHT RICE
MIXED GREEN SALAD WITH TOMATOES
CHINESE KUMQUATS AND ALMOND
   COOKIES
NEW ORLEANS COFFEE, TURKISH STYLE

CLAM   2 dozen clams (cherrystone or comparable)
BROTH   1 tablespoon olive oil
2 dashes paprika
1 teaspoon dried parsley
Whipped cream
Chopped fresh parsley

Place the clams over 9 to 10 cups of water in a steamer and sprinkle shells with olive oil, paprika, and dried parsley. Steam until open (discarding any unopened clams), remove clams from shells, and reserve for rice recipe which follows. Serve clam broth in bouillon cups, topped with whipped cream, and sprinkled with fresh parsley.

SUNDAY   ½ cup olive oil
NIGHT   ½ clove garlic, finely chopped
RICE   2 large onions, thinly sliced
Salt
Paprika
3 cups raw dry rice
5 cups chicken stock
4 pinches saffron
Curry

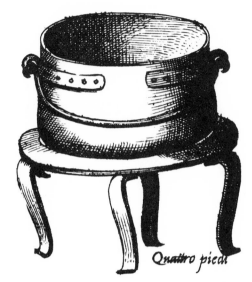

Quattro piedi

Turmeric

Monosodium glutamate (optional)

1 cup dried mushrooms, soaked in boiling water for about 10 minutes and simmered in a small amount of water and butter until tender

4 cups diced cooked lamb (preferably from leg)

4 cups diced cooked chicken

1 pound cooked shrimp

3 cups diced celery

1 tablespoon chopped parsley

1 cup thinly sliced canned bamboo shoots

½ cup white raisins

1 tablespoon slivers of lemon and orange peel

1 cup tangerine sections, cut into small pieces

Clams reserved from preceding recipe

Grated provolone cheese

Chopped toasted almonds

Shredded coconut

Heat the olive oil in a heavy skillet with a tight-fitting cover. Sauté the garlic, and before brown add onions and salt and paprika to taste. Before onions are brown add rice and stir until all grains are thoroughly mixed in oil. Heat the chicken stock and add it with saffron to the rice; boil for 1 minute. Add more salt, curry, turmeric, glutamate if wished, and mushrooms, and cook covered over very low heat (preferably an asbestos pad) for about 10 minutes. Add the lamb, chicken, and shrimp, and then the celery, parsley, bamboo shoots, raisins, peel, tangerine sections, and clams. Stir all and cook for another 10 minutes, or until rice is *al dente*. Serve with grated cheese, almonds, and shredded coconut in accompanying sweetmeat dishes.

Serves 10 to 12

Curry Powder

JOHN HOWAT
*American Paintings
and Sculpture*

A mild mixture that usually requires at least 1 tablespoon for most curry dishes. A sauce in which it is used should be simmered for about half an hour in order to develop the flavor (the key to a proper result).

> 5 teaspoons Sun Brand curry powder
> ¼ cup ground coriander
> 2 teaspoons red pepper flakes
> 1½ teaspoons saffron threads
> ½ teaspoon fennel seeds
> 1 teaspoon powdered fenugreek
> 1 teaspoon ground cardamom
> 1 tablespoon cumin seeds
> 1 tablespoon mustard powder
> 1 tablespoon poppy seeds
> 1 teaspoon ginger powder
> ½ teaspoon garlic powder
> 2 teaspoons turmeric
> 1 teaspoon peppercorns

Pulverize all ingredients in a mortar or a turret-top coffee grinder used to prepare European filter coffee. Thoroughly mix the powdered ingredients, and store in a tightly sealed screwtop jar.

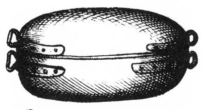

Conserva mezana

Watermelon Pickle

PHILIP HARCOURT
Drawings

Another recipe from Dean Walker, a former student intern in the department.

> 1 gallon watermelon rind squares or slices
> 1 teaspoon salt
> 1 teaspoon alum
> 1 pint vinegar
> 1 teaspoon whole cloves
> 4 pounds sugar
> 1 stick cinnamon

Place the watermelon rind, salt, and alum in an enamel bowl or kettle and cover with water; weight down. Let stand overnight and drain in the morning. Cover with clear water and boil until transparent. Combine the vinegar, cloves, sugar, and cinnamon, and heat to make a syrup. Cool and pour over watermelon. Baste for three mornings, then seal.

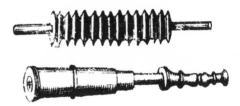

The Art of Making Kimchi

ANITA KOH
Ancient Near Eastern Art

Central to any Korean meal, along with a hearty soup and rice, is kimchi, a hot pickled cabbage that is sometimes known as "Korean soul food." Kimchi does have a distinctive smell! It also comes out differently every time, but you will soon master the art of making it. You will need two or three large jars with screw tops—apple juice jars do very well.

165

Salt

1 large Japanese cabbage (*hakusai*), or 2–3 large
  celery cabbages, washed and chopped into
  1-inch pieces

½ cup Oriental red pepper flakes

1 teaspoon sugar

2 large cloves garlic, chopped

1 teaspoon chopped *fresh* ginger

1 tablespoon Oriental salted baby shrimp
  (optional)

5–6 scallions, chopped in 1-inch pieces
  (including green tops)

Salt the pieces of cabbage and allow to sit in a large bowl until soft and flexible, but not brown (this can take from 4 hours to overnight, depending on the temperature). In the meantime blend pepper flakes, sugar, garlic, ginger, shrimp (if desired), and ½ cup of water into a thick, lumpy paste. Drain the cabbage, reserving the water, wash cabbage, and taste it to see if it has a slightly salty taste. If not, add more salt. Put about 1 cup of cabbage in the bottom of each jar, add a spoonful of the pepper paste, and then add some of the scallions. Repeat layers until jars are filled. Pack down the mixture firmly and cover with the water drained from the cabbage; if you do not have enough, use tap water. Cover the jars and let them sit overnight. Then refrigerate for 2 weeks.

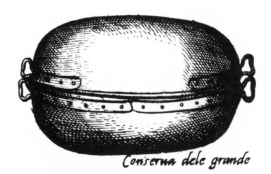

Conserna dele grando

Toasted Sesame Seeds

ANITA KOH
Ancient Near Eastern Art

Essential to Korean cooking, these are so good that you're sure to find yourself using them in other dishes too.

2 pounds white sesame seeds
Salt

Place the sesame seeds in an ungreased cast-iron skillet and toast over a very low flame, stirring occasionally, until they are a nice nutty brown. Add salt to taste, and crush with a spoon or in a blender. Store in an airtight container.

Crunchy Granola

ELIZABETH HAMMOND
European Paintings

Commercial dry cereals are transformed if mixed with a handful of this delicious mixture. Good alone too.

6 cups rolled oats
2 cups shredded coconut
2 cups wheat germ (untoasted)
1 cup sunflower seeds
1 cup sesame seeds
1½ cups chopped nuts (pecans, walnuts, almonds)
¾ cup honey
2 tablespoons oil
1 teaspoon vanilla

Preheat oven to 250°.

Mix all dry ingredients together. Melt the honey in ¾ cup hot water and add oil and vanilla. Combine with dry ingredients and spread in a well-oiled roasting pan. Roast for approximately 1 hour until brown, turning every 10 to 15 minutes to brown evenly. When cool put in an airtight container.

Ostreghine

Index

Designed by Peter Oldenburg
Composition and printing by The Stinehour Press, Lunenburg, Vermont
Bound by Spiral Binding, New York, New York